BEGUINE SPIRITUALITY

BEGUINE SPIRITUALITY

*Mystical Writings of Mechthild of Magdeburg,
Beatrice of Nazareth, and Hadewijch of Brabant*

Edited and introduced by
Fiona Bowie

Translated by Oliver Davies

Spiritual Classics
CROSSROAD · NEW YORK

1990

The Crossroad Publishing Company
370 Lexington Avenue, New York, N.Y. 10017

Printed in the United States of America

Library of Congress Cataloging-in-Publication Data

Beguine spirituality : mystical writings of Mechthild of
Magdeburg, Beatrice of Nazareth, and Hadewijch of
Brabant / edited and introduced by Fiona Bowie ; transla-
tions by Oliver Davies.
    p.   cm.
  Includes bibliographical references.
  ISBN 0-8245-0993-5
  1. Mysticism—Benelux countries.   2. Mysticism—Germany.
3. Mysticism—History—Middle Ages, 600-1500.   4. Beguines—
Spiritual life. I. Bowie, Fiona. II. Davies, Oliver.
III. Mechthild, of Magdeburg, ca. 1212-ca. 1282. Selections.
English. 1990. IV. Beatrijs, van Tienen, ca. 1200-1268.
Selections. English. 1990. V. Hadewijch, 13th cent.
Selections. English. 1990.
BV5082.2.B435 1990
248.2'2'09493—dc20

89-37397
CIP

To our mothers
with love and gratitude

The Beguinage, Bruges

The high gate keeps, it seems, nobody in
And the bridge leads contentedly out as well as within
And yet, it is certain that each and everyone
Is in the old Elm Court; they do not leave
Their houses, except to walk the short way
To church, in order that they may the better understand
Why there should be such love in them.

Rainer Maria Rilke, from *Neue Gedichte*

Contents

Preface

This anthology is very much a joint venture, a meeting of interests and skills. I am primarily responsible for Part One while my husband, Oliver Davies has taken care of the translations. The selection involved us both, and as the extracts have succeeded in appealing to our widely different tastes we very much hope that they will also touch a chord in many other readers. Our chief motivation in producing this anthology is to share our pleasure in reading the works of these exceptional mystics, and to draw them to the attention of a wider audience.

My thanks go to all those who have helped in any way with the production of this book. In particular I would like to thank my editor, Judith Longman, for her enthusiasm and encouragement. I am grateful to Nicola Hughes for her helpful comments on the manuscript, to Jean Williamson for preparing the map of Germany and the Low Countries, to Jane Thomas for her drawing of the beguinage at Bruges, to Bennie Callebaut and Jacquie Huys for acting as guides in Belgium, to Leopold van de Bussche and Dimitrij Bregant for their help in the final stages, and to the Cistercian sisters of the convent of Our Lady of Nazareth, who treasure the writings and memory of Beatrice and who provided us with the photograph of the modern stained glass window depicting their prioress which appears on the front cover. Finally, we would like to thank the Hofer family for the peace and hospitality necessary for completing this work.

Fiona Bowie
Mieders, Tyrol
November 1988

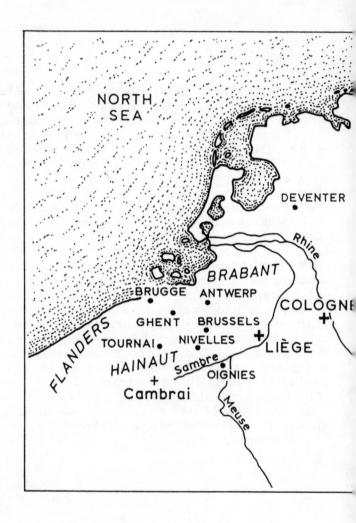

PART 1

Introduction

A Neglected Part of our Heritage

We can begin with the commandment to love: to love God with all our heart and all our soul and in all our deeds, to love ourselves in due measure and our fellow Christians as ourselves. To love God with all our heart means keeping our thoughts for ever fixed on him; to love him with our whole soul means with our very life, speaking always the truth about him; in all our deeds means that we should do everything for his sake. Loving ourselves in due measure means that we look for his will, not ours, to be done in us. Loving our fellows as ourselves means that we should do to them as we would have them do to us. All these aspects of the commandment are necessary for our salvation, and if we do not observe them, then grace will not live in us.

(*A Mirror for Simple Souls*, pp. 29–30)

To love God, to love our neighbour, to love ourselves. At various points in history people emerge who have made these central elements of the Christian message their own, and who are able to articulate them in a new way. The words above are those of a medieval lay woman, Marguerite Porete, a beguine from Hainaut in Belgium, whose own experience of a personal loving God transformed her life and overflowed in a desire to communicate that experience to others. All too often historians of Christian spirituality ignore the place of women writers within the mystical tradition. This is partly due to their 'invisibility' as women, but also because the personal, affective style of women's writing is judged inferior to that of the more systematic and theologically developed male writers of the period. The language of personal experience is, however, universal, and the strength, conviction and clarity of women's writings reach out to us across the centuries. In an individualistic world they remind us of the common bonds that form us into a community. In a world in search of unity, they stress the necessity of a personal choice of God. The goal in all ages remains the same: Love; love for God, love for our neighbour and for ourselves. We should not forget, however, that their message also demanded courage. The struggle to express and communicate an experience of God which is in essence beyond words had its dangers. Marguerite Porete was burned at the stake because of her reputed association with the heretical ideas of the 'Free Spirit'. Both Mechthild and Beatrice probably suffered from similar accusations, finding refuge only in a cloistered life. Hadewijch, no stranger to misunderstanding and acrimony, may also have come under suspicion of heresy. These women, nevertheless, felt compelled by a force greater than themselves to share their stories, to glorify God through their words, proclaiming that what God had accomplished in and through them is a gift available to all who truly choose to follow the way of love.

The extracts in this anthology come from three women who lived in North West Europe during the thirteenth century. All three are associated in various ways with the beguine movement. Both Hadewijch and Mechthild probably spent most of their adult lives in beguine communities, whereas Beatrice lived with beguines as a child before entering a Cistercian convent founded by her father. Hadewijch and Beatrice wrote in Flemish, and Mechthild in her Low German dialect. As an introduction to their writings, the following pages describe the environment in which these women lived, tracing the development of the beguine movement from its beginnings in the Low Countries at the end of the twelfth century to its decline (but not disappearance) some three hundred years later. An understanding of the place of women within late medieval European society, and of religious women and their writings in particular, is an essential prerequisite to a full appreciation of their works. It is to be hoped that these short extracts will succeed in communicating something of the richness of this much neglected part of our Christian heritage.

Women in the Medieval World

POWER AND CONTROL

Those who hold the reins of power in a society possess not only economic, legal and ecclesiastical advantages, but also control the way in which a society thinks about itself, determining the status of knowledge. Thus information about medieval society is largely determined by the interests of the nobility and the Church, the literate, governing elite of the medieval world who were 'the classes least familiar with the great mass of womankind'.[1] Women appear in this world through male eyes, as the romantic lady of courtly lovers, as the ideal obedient, patient and competent wife in manuals of instruction, as the perfect Virgin or cursed Eve of sermons and popular moral exemplars. It is only rarely and incidentally that we catch a glimpse of medieval women going about their daily lives, and discover something of their concerns.

If we make a distinction between power, seen as ability to achieve certain ends, and authority, hierarchical control over institutions, it is apparent that authority in medieval society was a male prerogative. The period from the twelfth to the fourteenth century saw a diminution in the power of aristocratic families and a rise in bureaucratic and institutional power. During the early Middle Ages women of noble families often wielded considerable public authority as abbesses and land holders, but by the twelfth century a concerted effort by church and civil authorities to exclude women from public life and confine them to the home or to the cloister had removed this avenue of female expression. Although women continued to be active commercially, as single women, as proxies for absent husbands and, above all, as widows, there was a general acceptance of the notion that formal authority was inconsistent with femininity.[2]

WOMEN AS WIVES

The age of marriage, sanctioned by both church and civil laws, was fourteen or fifteen for a boy and twelve for a girl. In practice, children of the landed classes were often married much younger, as pawns in a feudal game based on property. In feudal law a woman could inherit land, but on marriage her property merged with that of her husband. On widowhood a woman was entitled to a dower, a third of her late husband's property, and to the chattels or goods she had brought to the marriage. The primary purpose of marriage was not love or companionship, indeed, according to the courtly traditions of the aristocracy, love and marriage were inimical. A good wife was expected, according to the manual written by the Menagier of Paris, to be submissive to her husband at all times, obeying without question even the most nonsensical of instructions. Wife beating was sanctioned by canon law and was practised even in the highest circles of society. In the light of this unsavoury but prevalent attitude, the words of the twelfth-century theologian, Peter Lombard, provide a welcome contrast: 'God did not make woman from Adam's head, for she was not intended to be his ruler, nor from his feet, for she was not intended to be his slave, but from his side, for she was intended to be his companion and his friend.'[3]

A married woman of standing had considerable responsibilities and was expected to be practical and efficient, as well as obedient. The management of a medieval estate was a complex affair. The household consisted of a largely self-sufficient community which grew and cured its own food, provided its own clothes and maintained its lands, livestock and buildings. Women were responsible for all domestic arrangements, including care of the servants and sale of surplus produce. In noble circles, during her husband's frequent and often prolonged absence at court, on business or knightly service, a wife, as his representative, took over the management of the estate and defended her husband's interests in law or, if necessary, in battle. In widowhood a woman could continue to manage her late husband's affairs and take on new responsibilities in her own right, the legal limbo of marriage being replaced by a more independent status.

WORKING WOMEN

Women were active in crafts and trade in the middle ages, both as wives and daughters and as independent operators or *femmes soles*. Increased urbanisation and the development of craft and retail trades were a feature of northern European society, and women, as well as men, were drawn from the land to the growing industrial cities. Both girls and boys were apprenticed to trades and there were few areas in which women did not work:

> In this public realm women made and sold textiles, clothing, beer, bread, pottery, and other goods used both locally and abroad. They ran taverns and inns; they belonged to the guilds and confraternities; they brokered deals between visiting merchants and local manufacturers; they borrowed and lent money; they took oaths; they led religious movements; they ran charities; they joined popular political demonstrations; they sued and were sued; they learned and taught reading, writing, and arithmetic; they delivered babies for pay; and they dispensed medicine and medical advice.[4]

Public activity and visibility do not, however, connote authority and women remained in all aspects of life subordinate to the hierarchical power of men. However well qualified, women never earned 'the right to help govern their own professions, much less their own cities.'[5] The Cologne silk makers were exclusively women, yet their guild was run by men. Leiden's textile finishers included women as mistresses and apprentices until the craft was awarded political status, after which women were forbidden to train. Only a widow, on the death of her husband, became entitled to the male privileges of independent guild membership and the rights associated with the practice of a predominantly male trade.

WOMEN'S EDUCATION

The higher up the social scale, the more likely a woman was to acquire a formal education. Didactic works addressed to women give some indication of what was expected of them in the field of learning. Aristocratic ladies, caught up in the game of courtly love, were expected to become proficient at hawking, chess, story-telling, the art of witty repartee, singing, playing various musical instruments, reading and writing. Among the bourgeoisie there was a greater emphasis on Christian piety and good housekeeping. It was generally accepted that some nuns should be educated, chiefly those drawn from the top ranks of society, but there was less agreement as to the wisdom and necessity of learning for other women.

A few women were educated as boarders in nunneries or beguinages. Their learning was dependent upon that of their teachers which, in the case of nuns, was generally highest in the eleventh to thirteenth centuries, declining thereafter. The homes of great ladies sometimes employed a chaplain or beguine as children's tutor, forming small 'house schools' which catered for both sexes. The well educated and talented Hadewijch was probably educated at home by a private tutor. Records from thirteenth and fourteenth century Paris indicate that there were 'little schools' under the control of the Cantor of Notre Dame, which taught Latin to both girls and boys, and in the Low Countries some beguine schools catered for children of the poor, as well as the urban bourgeoisie. Nunneries sometimes specialised in a particular aspect of education; the Cistercians at La Ramée in Belgium, for example, acquired a reputation for teaching calligraphy and the copying of manuscripts. Women were not, however, admitted to higher levels of education and university training, and it was primarily the conventual life which fostered an atmosphere and provided an environment conducive to learning. Hildegard of Bingen (1098 –1179) produced extensive and much respected scientific, theological and medical works, and under its second abbess, Gertrude of Hackeborn (1251–1292), the Cistercian convent of Helfta, known as 'the crown of German women's convents', cultivated liberal and religious learning and produced some of the finest medieval women's literature.

ATTITUDES CONCERNING WOMEN

Quasi-scientific ideas affected attitudes towards women. People were thought to be composed of four elements or 'humours', hot, cold, moist and dry, the relative proportions of which determined an individual's personality. Women were said to contain a higher proportion of cold and wet humours, and were consequently more given to lust. The male world was seen as rational, belonging to the higher realms of the intellect and spirit, in contrast to the female world of matter, which was, by implication, inferior.

This intimate connection believed to exist between women and the world of matter should be borne in mind when reflecting upon the extreme asceticism of many women mystics. When the material world itself is seen as corrupt women are in danger of developing a negative attitude towards their bodies, which then become objects of hatred and contempt, deserving of mortification and neglect. It was primarily through identification with the human, incarnate Christ, in his tormented suffering, that the medieval female ascetic was empowered to assert her own humanity, believing it capable of redemption and transformation.

Women in the Medieval Church

MONASTIC REFORM AND THE *VITA APOSTOLICA*

Women invariably posed a problem for the medieval church, whether gathered in a Cistercian cloister or attracted to the mendicant preachers seeking to imitate the life of the apostles. The monastic reforms of the tenth and eleventh centuries, which resulted in the rapid spread of Benedictine and Cistercian monasteries, centred on Cluny and Citeaux in France, were essentially male oriented and hostile towards women. Evangelical preachers, such as Norbert of Xanten (*c.* 1085–1134), founder of the Premonstratensian canons and canonesses, or the mendicant friars who followed Francis of Assisi (c.1181–1226) and Dominic (1170–1221), attracted women but were unwilling to absorb them into their ranks. For the monastic male, women were regarded as a spiritual danger, while the friars' life of mendicancy and begging was inconceivable for women. The religious impulse, however, cannot be confined to one sex alone, and women continued to draw inspiration from the new religious currents and to seek accommodation within the existing orders.

NUNNERIES

It was only a hundred and fifty years after the foundation of the Benedictine monastery of Cluny in Burgundy that Hugh, its sixth abbot, established at Marcigny the first Cluniac monastery for women, intended primarily as a retreat for his mother and for the wives and daughters of men whom he had persuaded to become monks. Unlike the earlier double monasteries in England which were under the care of an abbess (such as Hild of Whitby, 614–680), the women at Marcigny were granted no say in the running of their affairs, the office of prioress being allotted to the Virgin Mary herself, and they were to be strictly enclosed lest 'in appearing in the world they either made others desire them, or saw things which they themselves desired'.[6]

The Benedictine and Cistercian nunneries which followed the establishment of Marcigny provided a solution to the nobility's problem of what to do with unwanted daughters, widows, and other well-born women, for whom marriage was neither desirable nor possible, and who could bring with them a sufficient dowry. This is not to suggest that all women entered monastic enclosures unwillingly, their popularity indicating that, despite the rigorous conditions which prevailed, a cloistered life presented an attractive alternative to marriage for many women. Many of these cloisters preserved their generally aristocratic character, although women of lesser birth were admitted to fulfil the function of servants within the nunneries.

As Benedictine, Cistercian and Premonstratensian nunneries continued to proliferate, the parent orders expressed profound misgivings about the presence of these women. They were commonly regarded as a drain on resources, a source of temptation for male clerics who ministered to them, and as a responsibility irrelevant to the monastic aims of their male founders. By the fifteenth century, despite frequent attempts to discourage their growth, women actually formed a majority of the cloistered religious, due in part to the lack of an alternative. Whereas men might become secular priests, monks or friars, women wishing to embrace a religious rule were invariably enclosed.

LAY MOVEMENTS

As the twelfth century progressed the impulse among lay women and men to seek an alternative to monastic enclosure as the only form of Christian witness gathered strength. Chastity, simplicity, poverty and manual labour were key elements of a new spirituality which found expression in many different forms. One of the earliest of these movements were the Tertiaries, a lay fraternity of the Humiliati in Lombardy, who were approved by the Pope in 1201. They were admired by Jacques of Vitry in 1216 as 'almost the only orthodox group in the heretical city of Milan'.[7] The Dominicans and Franciscans adopted a similar form of organization to the Humiliati with both lay and religious branches. Prominent among the laity in the Low Countries at this time were the holy women (*mulieres sanctae*) who became known as 'beguines'. They included both women living alone and in community and never formed a coherent group with a single leader or organizational structure. They promised to remain chaste while living as beguines, but were free to marry or to enter an established religious community. What united this disparate group of individuals was a desire to lead a committed Christian life, together with other women, without the constraints imposed by marriage or enclosure. This balance between the secular and religious life is well summed up by a later observer, John Malderus, Bishop of Antwerp (1563–1633) who noted:

. . . it was a common capacity of many pious women in Belgium to rejoice in excellence rather than promise it. They preferred to remain chaste perpetually than to vow perpetual chastity. Likewise they were more eager to obey than to vow obedience, to cultivate poverty by frugal use of their fortunes than to abandon everything at once: they might be the kinder to the poor if something were left. They preferred to submit daily, as it were, to obedience within the enclosure than to be confined once and for all. In constant spontaneity they found compensation for perpetual claustration.[8]

The Birth of a New Movement

THE ORIGIN OF THE TERM 'BEGUINE'

The term 'beguine' still evokes for many people the notion of heresy, and although its precise origin is not known, it may have originated as a derogatory term for a female heretic. People calling themselves beguines were first recorded in the twelfth century in the diocese of Liège in Belgium. One theory suggests that they were the successors of a group of pious women who had been inspired by the church reformer, Lambert le Bègue ('the stammerer'; d. 1177), who was falsely accused of belonging to an heretical sect known as the 'Apostles'.[9] The nickname 'le Bègue', from Old French *li Beges* or 'one dressed in grey', after the colour of the their grey penitential dress, was synonymous with 'heretic'. The Humiliati, a contemporary apostolic group in southern Europe, were similarly named after the colour of their clothes.[10]

A second possibility, less likely but no more flattering to the beguines, is that the term is derived from 'Albigensian', another heretical sect, named after the proponents of the Cathar heresy in the region of Albi in the South of France. Catharism posed a major threat to Christian orthodoxy in southern Europe from the twelfth to the late thirteenth century. Its adherents preached a dualistic theology of the separation of pure spirit from evil matter, declaring that the material world, including the body, sex and marriage were sinful, and that perfection involved the denial of one's sexual nature. They taught that if you cannot attain to the perfection of the celibate *perfecti* or 'pure ones' you might as well be promiscuous, as marriage merely gave a spurious respectability to what was an essentially sinful state. There is, however, no real link between the beguines and the Albigensians, and a Belgian beguine, Marie of Oignies (1177–1213), urged her great admirer and biographer, Jacques of Vitry, to become a preacher in the Albigensian Crusade.

A popular conception from the seventeenth century was that the beguines were founded by St Begga, a seventh century duchess of Brabant, who, along with Catherine of Alexandria (*c*.300), came to be regarded as a patroness of the beguines.

THE FIRST BEGUINES AND THEIR PRECURSORS

Enormously popular and influential in their time, the beguines could perhaps be described as the first European women's movement. The term beguine was applied to a variety of pious women who chose to lead communal lives of prayer and service.[11] Although some beguines remained with their parents or in their own homes, they often set up house together, referred to as a 'convent', sometimes in the vicinity of a hospital or leprosarium, or clustered around an established religious community. As the beguine movement gathered strength there was a tendency for these settlements, which became known as 'beguinages' (Flemish: *begijnhoven*) to increase in size and complexity. The women, who might be single, married or widowed, commonly made an informal vow to remain celibate while living as a beguine, but retained the use of private property. They were free to change their status and were not under the obligations of a monastic rule.

The appearance and development of the beguines was the result of a combination of demographic factors, changing social circumstances, and a new religious enthusiasm for the *vita apostolica*. There was a surplus of marriageable women and widows in the Low Countries, Germany and France, the areas in which the beguines were most numerous, due to local feuds, wars, crusades, and the large number of celibate secular and regular clergy. Many men never returned from the crusades or from other military exploits, while others became wandering mercenaries or bandits. The unmarried daughters and widows of higher rank often sought to enter a nunnery, as recluses, boarders or as professed nuns, but faced with the official hostility of the established orders towards new female recruits, women in some areas found this course of action closed to them. The Bishop of Liège, Hugo of Pierrepont (elected in 1200), took steps to prevent women seeking to enter convents in his diocese as recluses. In consequence, groups of women established themselves as unofficial recluses, often in their own homes, and without formal monastic affiliations.

The first beguines may have resembled the recluses, individuals and small groups of women of ecstatic temperament and common religious interests, but with no official status. It was these 'holy women', daughters of merchants and of the minor nobility, whom Lambert le Bègue, 'a fervent preacher of the new religion',[12] inspired, and who formed, around 1170–1175, one of the earliest groups of beguines. Other groups of women who became identified as beguines sprung up at Mont Cornillon in Huy in 1182, associated with a woman called Ivetta, at Williambroux near Nivelles in 1192, around Marie of Oignies, and in Nivelles itself in the same year. Contemporary observers generally reported positively on this new movement. Caesarius Heisterbach (c.1180–1240), for instance, praised the religious women of Liège, who remained in secular dress among ordinary people but who surpassed in charity those who were cloistered. 'In the midst of worldly people they were spiritual, in the midst of pleasure seekers they were pure and in the midst of noise and confusion they led a serene, eremetical life.'[13]

LIÈGE AND NIVELLES

The beguine way of life caught the imagination and answered the needs of many women in the twelfth and thirteenth centuries. The holy women of Liège were renowned for their good works, religious fervour and learning, and inspired others to adopt a similar way of life. Within a few years women calling themselves beguines were to be found throughout the Low Countries, in Germany, France, and as far afield as Sweden, Spain, Italy, Austria, Poland and Hungary.

One of the earliest beguine communities was at Nivelles in Brabant (Belgium), where a group of beguines lived together in a house in the parish of Saint Sepulchre. They were joined in around 1207 by a child of seven or eight years old called Ida. She lived with them for a year or so and then moved to another beguine house, before joining a Cistercian community at La Ramée at about sixteen years of age. A similar path was followed by Beatrice of Nazareth and both women acquired reputations for sanctity, based in part on the dissemination of their mystical writings.

By the middle of the thirteenth century Nivelles, according to the Dominican theologian Thomas of Cantimpré, possessed some two thousand beguines, drawn from Champagne, Germany and Flanders, as well as the towns and villages around Nivelles. Whatever the accuracy of the figure, the number must have accounted for a sizeable proportion of the unattached female population of the town.[14] We do know that by 1231 Nivelles had grown to the extent that ten new parishes were requested, and that the beguines here were generally well thought of by the Church's hierarchy.[15]

MARIE OF OIGNIES

A key figure in the development of the beguine movement was Marie of Oignies. Marie appears to have been a woman of remarkable determination with considerable charisma and powers of persuasion. Born in Nivelles in 1176/7, she was married at the age of fourteen to a young man chosen for her by her parents. Marie had already decided to follow a religious life and managed to convince her husband to join her in taking a vow of chastity, and to accompany her to a leper colony at Williambroux, where they devoted themselves to the service of the sick. In 1207, with the consent of her husband John,

Marie escaped from the growing number of followers who surrounded her to live as a lay sister at the little known Augustinian priory of St Nicholas at Oignies sur Sambre (Aiseau in Henegowen), near Namour.[16]

With her enthusiastic espousal of a simple, ascetic, devotional life, and her strong, charismatic personality, Marie became a focal point for the priory, and in particular for the lay women, including the mother and sisters of the prior, who lived nearby. This group of women, referred to as beguines, formed what might be thought of as one of the earliest examples of a beguinage. Jacques of Vitry (d. 1240), a French nobleman who first heard of Marie while a student in Paris, and who under her influence became a priest and canon of St Nicholas (and later a bishop, then cardinal and member of the Roman curia), painted a peaceful picture of the life of these women, assisting and consoling one another in their afflictions.[17] Another observer, Thomas of Cantimpré, who wrote a supplement to Jacques of Vitry's 'Life' of Marie of Oignies, recounts an incident which paints a slightly different picture, and indicates that Marie was perhaps not the easiest person to live with. On the feast of the Trinity in about the year 1210, the prior and all the other canons were out, leaving the church without a priest. The women were about to eat their midday meal when Marie, who was recognized as having the gift of prophesy, as well as a great devotion to the Eucharist, told them to wait as the prior would soon hold a service. The prior's mother, who as the oldest member of the community was accorded seniority among the beguines, was dumbfounded and ordered the sisters to sit down and eat, claiming that if her son did return he would be tired from his journey and would have no wish to celebrate mass. Not to be dissuaded, Marie went to the church and rang the bell. The prior arrived, and went straight to the altar without a word. Confused, the old woman left the table and after mass asked Marie to forgive her for her haste.[18]

The beguines at Oignies earned their living by manual work, or were supported by gifts and endowments. Marie, when not in church, is said to have spent her days quietly spinning, with her psalter propped up in front of her. After Marie's death (23

June 1213), the beguinage continued to develop, the women living in cottages built on land between the priory and the Sambre. But by 1250, when most of the relatives of the founding priors, who had been affected by the early days of intense piety, had died, the cardinal legate ordered the demolition of beguine houses as the occupants died 'since the beguines cannot be seen from such close range without great danger',[19] and the beguinage was relocated away from the priory in another part of the town. The last mention of a beguinage at Oignies is in 1352.

OFFICIAL RECOGNITION AND GROWING ACCLAIM

The first papal recognition of the new style of religious life followed by Marie of Oignies and the other *congregationes beguinarum disciplinatarum* (beguines living a common life) as opposed to the *beguinae singulariter in saeculo manentes* (individual holy women remaining in the world), was obtained by Jacques of Vitry from Pope Honorious III in 1216. The Fourth Lateran Council had just issued a decree prohibiting the foundation of new religious orders but Jacques of Vitry's argument that 'a valid vocation for want of dowry or material resources might not meet the requirements of an approved order'[20] secured a verbal approval for the new movement.

By the middle of the thirteenth century the reputation of the beguines was sufficiently established for an English monk, Matthew Paris, to refer to them in his Survey of Europe:

> At this time and especially in Germany, certain people – men and women, but especially women – have adopted a religious profession, though it is a light one. They call themselves 'religious', and they take a private vow of continence and simplicity of life, though they do not follow the Rule of any saint, nor are they as yet confined within a cloister. They have so multiplied within a short time that two thousand have been reported in Cologne and the neighbouring cities.[21]

The esteem in which this new style of religious life was held, by some at least, can be seen in the following story concerning the distinguished bishop of Lincoln, Robert Grosseteste, who, according to the English Franciscan, Thomas of Ecclestone,

> . . . one day preached a sermon to the Franciscans in which he extolled the life of begging as the highest kind of poverty next to heaven itself. But later in private he told the Franciscans that there was a still higher kind of poverty: this was to live by one's own labour 'like the beguines'. These holy people, he declared, had the most perfect and holy form of religious life because they lived by their own efforts and did not burden the world with their demands.[22]

The beguines also attracted some powerful patrons among the aristocracy, including Louis IX of France, who founded a beguinage in Paris, and his successors, and the Countesses Jeanne and Marguerite of Flanders.

CONSOLIDATION AND INCREASING COMPLEXITY

The observation made by Matthew Paris in 1243 that the beguines were not 'as yet' in a cloister expresses, despite his approbation, the uneasiness experienced by many clerics at the sight of independent women who could be classified as neither wives nor nuns. The transition from loose associations of individuals and small groups to communities following a more ordered and cloistered way of life was partly a response to the success of the movement, but also a form of protection in the face of official hostility. The Bull *Gloriam virginalem*, promulgated by Pope Gregory IX in 1233, was interpreted as sympathetic to the notion of beguine 'convents', or communal houses, and acted as a spur to their development.

The numbers of women housed in the beguine convents was often fewer than ten and almost never more than fifty, but the total number of beguine convents multiplied rapidly during the thirteenth and fourteenth centuries as new houses were established in all major urban centres throughout the Low Countries, Germany and in France. Between 1250 and 1350 a total of a hundred beguine houses, which together could house one thousand women, are said to have been founded in Cologne, the second largest north European city after Paris, with a population of around 30,000 at this time. Strasburg, a city of about 20,000 people in the fifteenth century, housed some six hundred beguines. Similar figures for other German cities attest the popularity of the beguine movement in that country.[23]

The *beguinae singulariter* continued to exist but were subject to increasing harassment and persecution, including the forfeiture of beguinal privileges. They were also said to be more prone to doctrinal errors and to lapses from the high moral standards for which the beguines were so admired. Whatever the truth of such accusations, and it is very difficult to determine their validity, beguines who persisted in supporting themselves, through a craft, by trade, begging or private income, outside a convent were accused of bringing the entire movement into disrepute.

The final stage of development in the Low Countries was the beguinage, which increasingly, although not entirely, replaced individuals and the smaller groups of beguines living together. It was a formidable institution comprising:

> a church, cemetery, hospital, public square, and streets and walks lined with convents for the younger sisters and pupils and individual houses for the older and well-to-do inhabitants. In the Great Beguinage at Ghent, with its walls and moats, there were at the beginning of the fourteenth century two churches, eighteen convents, over a hundred houses, a brewery, and infirmary.[24]

The larger beguinages in Flanders and Brabant were sometimes accorded the status of autonomous parishes. These beguine parishes were allowed secular privileges, including exemption from taxes, as well as ecclesiastical rights such as freedom from the jurisdiction of magistrates and the right to hold services during times of papal displeasure, known as an interdict, when normal ecclesiastical life was forbidden. The beguines' less numerous male counterparts, the beghards, were granted similar privileges and in addition were exempted from military service.

PERSECUTION AND DECLINE

Despite much popular support, the success of the beguines also earned them suspicion and hatred. There may well have been opposition from families whose daughters' choice of the beguine life of poverty, work and prayer was interpreted as an attempt to escape from lawful male authority and the duties of married life. Clerical opposition, fuelled by sometimes outspoken criticism of the Church and a distrust of beguine mystical theology, resulted in accusations of immorality and heresy, particularly associated with the supposed sect of the 'Free Spirit'. It appears that there were Christians who claimed that they had attained a state of perfection in which the moral law no longer applied to them, and in which the sacraments of the Church became unnecessary. As the Church became increasingly paranoid concerning the presence of heterodox teachings, and brutal in its attempts to eradicate those it conceived of as a threat, beguines and beghards, along with Jews, witches and various other sects, found themselves vulnerable and subject to frequent accusations of heresy, with often terrible consequences.

Widespread clerical persecution following the papal condemnation of the beguines at the Council of Vienne in 1311 seriously weakened the beguine movement, although in the Low Countries the beguinages, with their sympathetic patrons, afforded the beguines some protection, and they remained strongholds of the beguine way of life. By the fifteenth century, outside the Low Countries, beguine convents had become little more than charitable institutions, which were almost completely suppressed during the Protestant Reformation in the sixteenth century. The Belgian beguinages, however, experienced a second period of growth following the Counter-Reformation in the seventeenth century. The Great Beguinage in Leuven (Louvain, Belgium), for example, whose numbers in 1597 had fallen to 90, reached its peak a hundred years later with 298 beguines and eight novices. During this period many new houses and triumphalistic baroque churches were added to the beguinages.[25]

There were beguines in Cologne until the eighteenth century, when they were wiped out in another wave of suppression in the wake of the French Revolution. The beguinages in Belgium survived, in part through classification as medical rather than religious institutions, but they never recovered their former popularity. A gradual decline in numbers has occurred throughout the nineteenth and twentieth centuries, leaving today only a handful of beguines to remind us of their long and unique tradition.

Life as a Beguine

... the newly emancipated women religious were able to evolve a way of life hitherto unknown in the West, free from monastic enclosure, observing the rules which they themselves devised to meet the needs of individual communities, following lives of intense activity which might be devoted to prayer, to teaching and study, to charitable works, or to all three.[26]

A movement, rather than an order, there was no single style or pattern of beguine life. A predisposition towards an active or a contemplative vocation, the desire to live in one's own home, in a communal setting or in a large beguinage, as well as the period and place, would all have affected the day to day life of a beguine.

THE INDIVIDUAL BEGUINE

In the early days of the beguine movement most of the women lived scattered in different parts of a town or city, coming together daily at particular churches or chapels for mass. They might be recognized as a distinct community despite the lack of a common rule or residence, although the unregulated nature of their life seldom met with enthusiasm from the ecclesiastical authorities.

There was a tendency for beguines to cluster around an institution, such as a priory[27] or hospital, and they would often buy and sell property in order to live with or near other beguines, leaving these houses in their wills to other female relatives who wished to follow the same pattern of life. Records of conveyance in Cologne indicate the scale of such activity, the number of property transactions involving beguines reaching a peak of 164 in 1309, by which time the city also boasted twenty-two beguine convents.[28]

BEGUINE CONVENTS

The convents each developed their own house rules, often intricate and exhaustive in their detail, which stipulated the activities to be followed at each moment of the day; the time allotted to prayer, to work, to silence and to entertainment, and regulating the movement of visitors and movements outside the convent. How far these regulations were ever followed is, of course, another matter. The purpose of such rules was to provide an environment of quiet and prayerful contemplation, while earning a living through manual work or service. The mistress of the convent was chosen for her maturity and wisdom, and had the task of overseeing the affairs of the convent in everything pertaining to the lives of her sisters.

THE BEGUINAGE

In the Low Countries beguines were frequently granted land on which to build their own communities. The majority of these settlements, which varied in size from a small hamlet to a 'city within a city', and which existed in almost every town, were built between 1230 and 1300, and were sometimes granted the status of a separate parish. In a fully developed beguinage, such as those in Leuven or Ghent, with its numerous houses, convents, schools and hospitals, a common pattern of organization emerged. Each beguinage appointed one or more grand mistresses, who administered the beguinage with the help of a council of other mistresses, each with a specific function. Beguines promised to obey the grand mistress, the statutes of the beguinage and the ecclesiastical authorities. They agreed not to leave the beguinage without permission, to forego the choice of residence or work, and to live a simple and celibate life for the duration of their residence.

Aspiring beguines lived under the wing of an older beguine mistress for one to two years before taking the habit of a beguine. The beguine habit evolved only slowly. In the early days beguines dressed much as other women, although more simply, avoiding expensive cloth and ornamentation, but eventually a grey or blue habit, which from the seventeenth century became black with a white head covering, was adopted. If the 'novice mistress' and council considered the applicant suited to beguine life the candidate would make a simple promise to 'offer themselves to Christ', to 'live religiously all their lives' or 'to serve the Lord Jesus Christ in the habit of a beguine'.[29] In some cases they undertook to remain in the beguinage for at least six years, or until the age of thirty. In practice many women probably spent the greater part of their lives within a beguinage or beguine convent, particularly from the middle of the thirteenth century when the church authorities expressed their disapproval of beguines and other religiously-minded women living on their own.

RELIGIOUS LIFE

Religious observance consisted of daily attendance at mass and at the saying of the Divine Office, prescribed prayers in honour of the Virgin, the Passion, for souls and for benefactors, meditational readings and lectures, communal penances and confession at fortnightly or monthly intervals. The feasts and vigils of the Virgin and of other festivals were observed and were occasions of recollection during which they remained within the beguinage and received Holy Communion.

The beguines sought out priests sympathetic to their aims as spiritual directors and chaplains, and Dominican friars frequently acted in this capacity, sometimes appointed by the ecclesiastical authorities specifically as chaplains to a beguinage. There were also close links with Cistercian houses and, despite official disapproval or lack of interest, at a local level the Cistercian abbots often supported the development of women's communities, be they beguinages or nunneries.

THE INHABITANTS AND PROPERTY OF A BEGUINAGE

Within the beguinage were houses for widows or single women, who paid a rent, much as convents took in boarders from among the nobility (providing a form of medieval 'sheltered housing'), and who presumably enjoyed the atmosphere of simple and wholesome piety and the company of other women. There were also frequently mothers, sisters and other female relatives of beguines present. None of these women would wear the beguine habit and they were not bound by the regulations of the beguinage.

Some of the houses in a beguinage would be built by women who wished to join the community, or by families who wanted to provide for a daughter or some other female relative. Other houses or convents were endowed by wealthy patrons for poor beguines. Houses could be left by will to named women with the proviso that they accepted the beguine way of life, or rented out to other beguines by the beguinage. No property, once built within the confines of a beguinage, could then be alienated from it.

Beguines did not take a vow of poverty and could retain personal property. In fact, a girl wishing to join a beguinage had to bring with her basic household goods and utensils. Regulations concerning what could be taken out of a beguinage if a woman wished to leave varied, but if a woman was dismissed for misconduct she forfeited everything except the clothes she was wearing. In practice, records indicate that women retained a considerable degree of discretion in the management of their private affairs. They were, however, expected to live modestly, and an annual visitation by the grand mistress to each of the houses and convents determined that its inhabitants lived neither too luxuriously nor, interestingly, too simply. While reacting against the wealth and ostentation of secular society, the beguines did not see poverty as an end in itself, rather they encouraged the development of the virtues of charity, humility and companionship.

EARNING A LIVING

The activities of beguines were various. Although beguinages attracted some endowments, and some individuals had private means, they had to be self-supporting. Involvement in the textile industry was common, and beguinages were often sited on the outskirts of a city with access to fields and running water, necessary for the treatment of cloth, one of their main sources of income. Many beguines were occupied with weaving, bleaching, carding and that quintessentially female occupation, spinning, as well as dressmaking, lace work and the embroidery of church vestments.

Beguine involvement in industries such as cloth-making often brought them into conflict with the town guilds, which sought to restrict trade to their members and resented the beguines' privileges in the buying and selling of materials and their ability to avoid apprenticeships. In order to avert a clash of interests, particularly in the fourteenth and fifteenth centuries as the guilds increased their hold over civic life, forced or voluntary regulation of beguine industry became necessary, limiting the type and quantity of the work they could do and reducing the profitability of their enterprises.

There was a fundamental orientation towards the poor and sick, and beguines worked in hospitals, visited the sick in their homes and established infirmaries. The two main charitable institutions of the beguinage, the Infirmary and the Table of the Holy Spirit, provided permanent care for ill, poor and elderly beguines. A beguine supported by one of these institutions would leave it her property when she died, by way of compensation. Wealthier beguines and secular patrons supported these charities through gifts and endowments.

Teaching was another characteristic activity. In contrast to the nunneries, education was not confined to the children of the nobility and poor schools were established, as well as those catering for the urban middle class and gentry. Beatrice of Nazareth and Ida of Nivelles were both educated by beguines and would have lived in a beguine house with their mistress during the period of their education.

A census taken in 1646 of the Great Beguinage in Leuven

mentions a total of 272 children living in about sixty different houses (out of a total of around a hundred), the number of children exceeding that of beguines. Their ages ranged from five to sixteen and they lived in groups varying in size from three to twelve children, together with their mistress or mistresses. Other children came in daily from the town to receive lessons. The children were taught to read, write and to perform handwork, and must have resembled apprentices in many respects. Older beguines sometimes complained that their peace was shattered by the sound of children playing in the gardens, streets and rivers of the beguinage, and as one observer commented, the beguinage can seldom have been as peaceful as it is today![30]

Other beguines took in laundry for students and townspeople, or worked as housekeepers for priests. Beguines were also popular as servants to the bourgeoisie. The fourteenth-century author of the *Menagier de Paris* employed a beguine, known as Dame Alice, to instruct his young wife in household management and the supervision of the servants.

A COMMUNITY OF WOMEN

Although the beguines at times suffered considerable hardship, through persecution and confiscation of their property (by both ecclesiastical and secular powers), and were not immune from the social and political upheavals around them (beguinages were used as billets for Spanish soldiers, together with their families, servants and livestock, in the sixteenth century), they nevertheless achieved a life remarkable for its balance and simplicity. They lived neither in luxury nor in destitution, in isolation nor in overdependence. They avoided institutionalization while reaping the benefits of community living and combined manual work and prayer, contemplation and caring in a way which strikes us with its practicality and goodness. One of the most remarkable features of the beguine life is the way in which they avoided claustration or absorption into a third order, preserving their autonomy and the essential lay character of their religious vocation.

The beguines, as an independent community of women,

posed a challenge to society's basic definition of female roles. Classified neither as nuns nor as wives and mothers, they could not easily be labelled or fitted into existing categories. The power to avoid traditional stereotypes, to discover their own potential and to compose and control their own institutions, however tenuous, culturally conditioned and vulnerable these attempts may have been, represent the great strength and originality of the beguine movement.

Beguine Spirituality

BEGUINE PIETY

The diocese of Liège, towards the end of the twelfth century, witnessed an upsurge in popular piety, particularly among women, which emphasized the humanity and passion of Christ, and which was characterized by the espousal of poverty, chastity and devotion to the Eucharist, regarded as the culmination of a mystical marriage between the soul and its heavenly Bridegroom. Identification with Christ in his suffering often took the form of an intense asceticism, prolonged fasts, self-mortification, and accompanying visionary and ecstatic states. Marie of Oignies, possibly the first stigmatist,[31] was a proponent of this type of spirituality, although by no means unique.

The Flemish mystic, Beatrice of Nazareth, based her spirituality on an extreme ascetic imitation of Christ's sufferings, accompanied by an intense Eucharistic devotion. According to her biographer her longing to receive Christ in the Eucharist could occasion a near-fatal bleeding, while reception of the Eucharist might engender physical collapse.[32] Gertrude van Oosten, a Dutch beguine (d. 1358), was renowned for her 'frequent ecstasy, revelations and predictions, cognizance of the devil, fervent meditation on the passion, and reception of the stigmata',[33] although we are told by her biographer that out of fear of vanity and presumption she asked to have the stigmata removed. Her obedience to the Church and frequent confessions and communion are also emphasized, to remove any hint of heterodoxy.

BEGUINE PRAGMATISM

Although a visionary, ecstatic temperament seems to have been a prerequisite for mystical writing, and Eucharistic devotion continued to mark beguine spirituality, the rules and statutes express a more pragmatic element in beguine spiritual life. The visionary who remained in a cataleptic trance all day could not work and was consequently a burden to her sisters. The precocious Christine of Stommeln (1242–1312), who as a girl ran away from her parental home to live among beguines in Cologne, received a cool reception. 'The claim that demons were plaguing her merely provoked smiles and drew forth from the extra-regulars comments on mental derangement or charges of feigned holiness',[34] and the beguines urged her to return to her parents.

Female mystics indulging in exaggerated ecstasies were often encouraged, however, wittingly or otherwise, by their male confessors and by the attention and expectations of their admirers. Peter of Gothland, a Dominican priest who recorded Christine of Stommeln's *Vita* and *Acta*, was much impressed by her ecstasies and, as a young friar, was encouraged by his superior to witness them. Holy women thought to possess prophetic or other supernatural gifts attracted the curious and hopeful, religious and lay, from far and near.

STRATEGIES FOR WOMEN

Why should some women, leading otherwise useful, independent lives, choose to follow a path which leads to apparent physical disintegration? One answer lies in an appraisal of the strategies open to women. In a society which undervalues female perceptions and accords women little authority, mystical or ecstatic experiences enable a woman to transcend the normal boundaries of her existence and to claim direct inspiration from God. This power is often used to good effect, providing a woman with a platform from which to enter and challenge the male world. The medieval mystics Hildegard of Bingen (1098–1179), and Catherine of Siena (c. 1347–1380), for example, were able to act effectively in the public realm by claiming divine authority for their words and actions. It was the conviction that they were in communion with God which gave Marguerite Porete and Mechthild of Magdeburg the courage to criticize those in the Church who fell short of the mission entrusted to them.

The extreme and often bizarre behaviour of women mystics, annoying at times to their companions and embarrassing to the visionary herself, was interpreted as a teaching for others, illustrating in an exaggerated form the path of Christian piety. Elizabeth Petroff, however, sees 'the violent crying of Margery Kempe, Marie of Oignies and Angela of Foligno as the inarticulate cry of one needing a voice, needing to have words in a world that would deny that voice'. These three women were all married, 'which made them unlikely candidates as images of purity and sanctity', and all three depended on men to write their words for them.[35] In some cases the cathartic effects of physical collapse enabled the woman mystic to reach a point of equilibrium, and eventually fullness of health, although we should not deny the possibility of spiritual growth without psychological wholeness.

STAGES OF VISIONARY ACTIVITY

Petroff describes four stages of visionary activity, elements of which are apparent among beguine mystics and visionaries. The first stage is that of purgation, in which the visionary focuses on the need to do penance for her past or present sins. We are told by Jacques of Vitry that Marie of Oignies, filled with horror at what she imagined to be the carnal pleasures of her past life,

> began to afflict herself and she found no rest in spirit until, by means of extraordinary bodily chastisement, she had made up for all the pleasures she had experienced in the

past. In vehemence of spirit, almost as if she were inebri-
ated, she began to loathe her body when she compared it
to the sweetness of the Paschal Lamb and, with a knife, in
error she cut out a large piece of her flesh which, from
embarrassment, she buried in the earth.[36]

Similarly, Mechthild, a beguine from Magdeburg in Germany,
tells us that 'with the weapons of my soul I so painfully
conquered the body that for twenty years I was never but tired,
ill and weak, first from remorse and sorrow, then from good
desires and spiritual effort. Thereafter were many days of
bodily illness'.[37]

The second stage of visionary activity is marked by a turning
away from self towards others, and manifests itself in concern
for their spiritual welfare, a concern so apparent in the letters
of Hadewijch to her young beguines. The visionary is often
made aware of the spiritual state of others, and her insights
mark her out as a spiritual authority, giving her the confidence
to act outside traditional female stereotypes. Hildegard of
Bingen, whose utterances were accorded papal recognition,
was not afraid to address herself to the great problems of her
day, nor to tell emperors and other leading figures how they
should act.

A third stage is described as that of doctrinal visions which
set in motion a dialogue between the visionary and her confessor and which provide visual parables for use as teaching
aids in giving spiritual guidance to others. When Mechthild
of Magdeburg took the step of accepting her illness from the
hands of God and confided in her confessor, she discovered
within herself the ability to describe her experiences in writing,
producing some of the most haunting and lyrical mystical
prose we possess.

The fourth stage is characterized by devotional visions aris-
ing from the imaginative meditation on the life of Christ and
the Virgin. The Middle Ages saw an increased realism in
religious art and preaching, and, apart from repetitive prayer,
imaginative meditation was often the only form of devotional
exercise available to those who were unable to read Latin.
Devotional meditations based on gospel stories and pious

legends, or on the liturgical calendar, are the usual sources of visionary images. Jacques of Vitry says of Marie of Oignies:

> He manifested himself to Marie in a form which was in keeping with the feast. Thus he showed himself at the Nativity as though he were a baby sucking at the breasts of the Virgin Mary or crying in his cradle, and then she was drawn to him in love just as if he had been her own baby. In this way the various feasts took on new interest according to how he manifested himself and each caused a different emotional state.[38]

It was particularly in meditation on the suffering of Christ, that the visionary was able to identify and come to terms with her own suffering, with the sense of frustration and impotence inherent in being a woman in a man's world. Beatrice of Nazareth, after many years of ascetic practices designed to imitate the physical sufferings of Christ, found that reception of the Eucharist restored her health and enabled her to look beyond her own concerns to the needs of others. She began to serve the sick and poor beyond the walls of the convent, and even defended criminals before the local judge.[39]

EVALUATING BEGUINE SPIRITUALITY

Not all beguines were visionaries or mystics and, in particular from the fourteenth century, such behaviour may well have been frowned upon. Nevertheless, the form of popular female spirituality which gave rise to the beguines admired ecstatic and other para-mystical experiences which today would be considered psychotic rather than saintly. How then are we to evaluate such phenomena? One possibility is to see beguine visionaries as women who conformed to the expectations of the medieval holy woman. Encouraged by over-credulous clergy and keen to emulate those held up as paragons of virtue, women denied their sexuality, repressed their emotional and intellectual gifts and abused their bodies through fasting, sleep deprivation and physical penances, such as the wearing of coarse clothing next to the skin. Their reward came in the form of periods of altered consciousness, in which they often felt themselves to be particularly close to God, and the approbation of the Church.

A second perspective would be to regard these visionaries as women who succeed in utilizing the limited resources available to them to achieve certain spiritual and material goals. Debarred direct access to the public world, their illnesses and visions become a vehicle for asserting their authority. By denying their own intelligence, strength and creative powers, they can claim divine inspiration for their words and actions. Medieval hagiography frequently stresses the holy person's lack of formal education and their reliance on the Holy Spirit, as a way of authenticating their experience and disarming potential opponents.

A third way of viewing beguine visionary, ecstatic behaviour is to regard it as a response to the reality of living as a woman in a male-oriented world. Denied the means to express and fulfil her ambitions and realize her capacities, the visionary turns her energies inwards. Marie of Oignies felt the call to preach and longed to imitate Christ as an itinerant beggar. Persuaded by her friends that begging was unseemly for a woman, and forbidden by canon law to preach, she had to live out her desires vicariously through Jacques of Vitry. Thérèse of Lisieux felt a vocation to the priesthood and longed to become a missionary, but as an enclosed nun turned her ambitions into a desire for physical martyrdom through an early death, thanking God at the end of her short life that she would die before the age at which, as a man, she might have been ordained to the priesthood.

Elements of all three explanations are probably necessary for coming to terms with beguine (and female) ecstatic experience. We should not, however, lose sight of the fact that even in its most extreme manifestations, beguine visionary activity combined with manual labour and a concern for the sick and the poor. As the beguine visionary, Hadewijch, continually reminded her young beguines, 'Be good to those who have need of you, devoted toward the sick, generous with the poor, and recollected in spirit beyond the reach of all creatures.'[40]

IS THERE A DISTINCTIVE FEMALE SPIRITUALITY?

Caroline Walker Bynum identifies three main elements in medieval women's religious experience which can be described as characteristically female. The first is a tendency for women to regard institutional structures as secondary and to place less emphasis on the formal organizational side of religious life. Many women wandered from one community to another, in and out of beguinages, nunneries and family life, making it difficult, in many cases, to ascribe them to any particular group, and she suggests that:

> The very fact that male chroniclers felt that they ought to tell the story of the founding of the beguines as if the 'order' had a leader and a rule like those of contemporary monastic or mendicant orders suggests that women's more informal arrangements for giving religious significance to ordinary life seemed odd and dangerous to male sensibilities.[41]

The life trajectories of medieval women saints and mystics seem to be less marked by sudden and dramatic conversions and reversals than those of their male counterparts. A high proportion of female saints are recorded as having decided on a religious life in early childhood, and grew gradually into their vocation through adolescence. The lives of male saints, by contrast, tell of 'abrupt adolescent conversions, involving renunciation of wealth, power, marriage and sexuality'.[42] This, Bynum suggests, is partly due to the greater ability of medieval men to determine the shape of their lives, and partly because women tended to use their ordinary experiences of powerlessness, service, sexuality, disease and nurturing as 'symbols into which they poured ever deeper and more paradoxical meanings'. Both men and women tended to see female saints as models of suffering, male saints as models of action.[43]

A third difference apparent in the writings and 'lives' of medieval men and women, despite many common themes, is the female inclination towards mysticism and para-mystical phenomena, such as trances, stigmata or levitation. Women's reputations for holiness were often 'based on supernatural charismatic authority, especially visions and supernatural signs',[44] and extreme penitential asceticism was often re-garded as a mark of sanctity. There are also certain recurrent devotional themes such as a devotion to the Eucharist and to the sacred heart of Jesus, visions of cradling or suckling the infant Christ, mystical union with Jesus as a beautiful bridegroom, and identification with Christ in his agony on the cross.

Finally, the place of visions is central in women's religious writing, inspiring confidence in the recipient and others, tapping springs of creativity, providing insights which can then be used as a source of teaching, transforming self-understanding and enabling the visionary to transform the world around her.

Critics, Mystics or Heretics?

WOMEN AS HERETICS

In 1236 a beguine named Aleydis[45] was executed on a charge of heresy. The public outcry caused by her burning may have deterred the authorities from pressing charges against other beguines, but she was not the only beguine to suffer at the hands of the Inquisition. Both beguines, and their male coun-terparts the beghards, were arrested for heresy at Colmar and Basle in 1290 and in 1310 Margarete Porete was burned in Paris. Hadewijch, Ida of Nivelles and Mechthild of Magdeburg all seemed to have 'suffered much from persecutions aroused by slanderous tongues'.[46] So were the beguines heretics or merely the victims of a 'subtle case of misunderstanding, in which genuine grounds for disquiet combined with suspicious conservatism and the persecuting mentality to smear pious, unprotected groups'?[47]

Heresy, defined as 'whatever the papacy explicitly or im-plicitly condemned during the period'[48] was endemic in the Middle Ages. Women were prominent in Catharism (from the Greek, *katharos*, 'pure'), which offered them a higher status than did the Catholic Church, but beguines, such as Marie of Oignies, actually took a firm stand against the Cathars (Albigensians), and when suspicion of heresy fell on beguines or beghards it was most often in connection with a supposed sect known as the 'Free Spirit'. Followers of the Free Spirit were thought to repudiate the Church and its sacraments, believing themselves to be so one with God that the moral law and normal means of grace no longer applied to them. A devotee could therefore act as he or she liked, being beyond the constraints of church discipline or ethical considerations.

CONDEMNATION AND CONTROL

In an attempt to root out the heresy of the Free Spirit a general ecumenical council under Pope Clement V, which met at Vienne between 1311 and 1312, promulgated a Bull, *Cum de quibusdam mulieribus*, calling on beguines to abandon their way of life. A second Bull known as *Ad nostrum* referred to the beguines and beghards as an 'abominable sect' on account of their following of the Free Spirit. Earlier councils at Lyons in 1274 and at Mainz in 1310, among others, had already expressed a distrust of fringe communities, and at Mainz the German beghards had been accused of heresy. The grounds on which the Council of Vienne condemned the beguines indicate the extent to which, due to their ambiguous status, they were perceived as threatening:

> We have been told that certain women commonly called Beguines, afflicted by a kind of madness, discuss the Holy Trinity and the divine essence, and express opinions on matters of faith and sacraments contrary to the catholic faith, deceiving many simple people. Since these women promise no obedience to anyone and do not renounce their property or profess an approved Rule, they are certainly not 're-ligious', although they wear a habit and are associated with such religious orders as they find congenial . . . We have therefore decided and decreed with the approval of the Council that their way of life is to be permanently forbidden and altogether excluded from the Church of God.[49]

There was, however, a let-out clause at the end of the decree, which claimed that this condemnation was not intended 'to forbid any faithful women from living as the Lord shall inspire them, provided they wish to live a life of penance and to serve God in humility, even if they have taken no vow of chastity, but live chastely together in their lodgings'.[50] This apparent contradiction may to some extent express the tension between the local hierarchy, often extremely hostile to the beguines, and the papacy, trying to hold the Church together and to prevent schism.

In the wake of the Council of Vienne the tide of ecclesiastical opinion turned decisively against the beguines and beghards. Whereas earlier papal legates and members of the aristocracy had extended protection to beguine communities, by the fourteenth century such support was not always sufficient to protect them from their enemies. In 1318 the Archbishop of Cologne, Henry of Virnebourg, reacted to the Council's Bull by ordering the dissolution of all beguine associations and their integration into Orders approved by the Pope.[51] In the persecution of beguine and other lay groups that followed the Clementine decrees, beguines and recluses of many years standing were deprived of their property, forced to relinquish their grey habits and, in some cases, persuaded to marry. It was undoubtedly a frightening and humiliating experience for many, but the patience and fortitude of these women earned them the praise of contemporary chroniclers.

As a result of pleas from beguines and their supporters that they were being unfairly punished Pope John XXII, Clement V's successor, issued in 1318 the Bull *Ratio recta*, which was aimed at defending the beguines who 'still lead irreproachable lives and do not adhere to heresies' and which ordered church authorities to restore confiscated beguine property.

Throughout the fourteenth century local and papal decrees, designed to control the beguines by enclosing them in convents, alternated with attempts to protect legitimate beguines and their property. Whereas previously the beguines had been widely regarded as a bulwark against heresy, a century later anyone pursuing a religious life outside the cloister was automatically suspected of heretical intent, and in 1421 Martin V ordered the Archbishop of Cologne 'to search out and destroy any small convents of persons living under the cloak of religion without a definite Rule'.[52]

The fear of heresy may have been genuine but politics and pique seem to have played a part in the persecution of the beguines. Their identification with the Friars was, in some cases, enough to earn the beguines the hatred of the secular clergy, who perceived a challenge to their own authority. The freedom of beguines from conventional ties and espousal of poverty, together with their mystical claims, also aroused suspicion and envy. The fury of some male clergy at the sight of independent women is well expressed by Bishop Bruno of Olmütz in East Germany who complained to the Pope in 1273 that the beguines followed no approved rule, 'used their liberty as a veil of wickedness in order to escape the yoke of obedience to their priests and the coercion of marital bonds and, above all, assumed the status of widowhood against the express authority of the Apostle who approved no widows under the age of sixty.' All beguines, according to Bishop Bruno, should be either 'married or thrust into an approved Order'.[53] Bishop Bruno, we can surmise, was not alone in locating the chief source of complaint against the beguines in the fact that they were women who declined to adopt the roles mapped out for them by society. It was only in the Low Countries and Northern France, where the beguinage was most fully developed, that beguines found the necessary peace and protection to pursue their way of life with both hierarchical approval and a minimum of interference.

MARGUERITE PORETE AND THE HERESY OF THE FREE SPIRIT

What then were the grounds for the charges of heresy levelled against the beguines? If the real reasons behind their persecution and condemnation owed much to the hidden agenda of misogyny and fear of female independence, exacerbated by often trenchant criticism of the institutional church and its ministers, officially at least it was beguine mysticism which provided the ammunition for the Inquisition.

We have in the case of Marguerite Porete, who was executed

on a charge of heretical mysticism in 1310, the work on which she stood accused, thus allowing us to judge the substance of the charge. The normal practice was for banned copies of a heretic's work to be destroyed, but Marguerite Porete's mystical testimony, *A Mirror for Simple Souls* continued to circulate anonymously in monasteries and convents in both the original French and in Latin and English translations.

Marguerite's work had previously been condemned by Guy II, Bishop of Cambrai (Belgium), sometime between 1296 and 1306, and then in around 1307 she was arrested by the new Bishop of Cambrai, Philip of Marigny, on a charge of spreading heresy 'among the simple people and beghards'[54] through *A Mirror for Simple Souls*. Marguerite was taken to Paris for interrogation but refused to answer her accusors. Because of her previous condemnation she was considered guilty of a relapse and on the strength of selective extracts taken from her book was found guilty of heresy and burned.

Hainaut, the area from which Marguerite came, is not far from Nivelles and Oignies, for over a hundred years a centre of beguine mystical piety, and Marguerite's *Mirror* shares many features in common with the work of other beguines from the Low Countries. It was written in the vernacular and was an attempt to describe a personal mystical experience of union with God in the form of a dialogue between love and the soul in which the soul progresses through seven states of grace. The language which gave rise to suspicion concerned the fifth and sixth states in which the 'annihilated' or 'liberated' soul is united with God.

> The soul at the highest stage of her perfection and nearest the dark night is beyond noticing the rules of the Church. She is commanded by pure love, which is a higher mistress than what we call 'charitable works'. She has passed so far beyond the works of virtue that she longer knows what they are about – but yet she has assimilated them to the point where they are part of her, the Church cannot control her – the Church here being understood as mainly to do with those who live in fear of the Lord, which is one of the gifts of the Holy Spirit.[55]

It is easy to see how language such as this, which talked about the soul's farewell to virtues, with its hints of anticlericalism, could appear antinomian.[56] Although the *Mirror* is similar in style and content to the writings of contemporary female mystics, her position as a beguine made Marguerite Porete particularly vulnerable. Ida of Nivelles, a century before Marguerite, had been charged with quietism, the complete and passive abandonment of self and will to God, but her life and rule as a Cistercian nun protected her. As one historian observes, 'What might have been possible in an established nunnery, without publicity, appeared not to be allowed to a beguine who wanted to propagate her work', and he concludes that:

> Heresy, then, in this case, if it existed at all, was of special character, concerned solely with the condition of mystical adepts at an advanced stage of perfection; there was no advocacy of libertarianism and disregard of the moral law for anyone, and the accusations against Porete gave an unfair picture of her views.[57]

Although there were, in all probability, people calling themselves beguines, or referred to as such by others, whose teaching or writing could not be contained within orthodox Christian doctrine, the notion that the beguines harboured a sect called the Free Spirit or propagated libertarian teachings is certainly distorted. Recent scholars have questioned the very existence of an organized sect, corresponding to the heretical propositions in the inquisitors' handbook, and it is tempting to conclude that 'All that really existed were individual mystics in communication with like-minded friends and followers on an informal basis, some of whom wrote or said some dangerous or extravagant things.'[58]

VIRGIN, MARTYR, MYSTIC, WITCH

Women religious in the Western tradition have been required to be virgin, martyr and mystic, but these three elements contain a fourth: 'The holy saint was also seen as frightening and castrating to men. Underneath the praise of her holiness, it is possible that the man who told her story saw the witch.'[59]

Male fear of this fourth element, the female power beneath the surface of suppliant piety, endangers women. Challenged in their assumptions of superiority, order and control, men can perceive female power as a threat and it is the most vulnerable women who suffer as a result. It is no accident that beguines were regarded with ambivalence and frequently portrayed as libertarians – the mirror image of the virgin – and associated with the antinomianism thought to be characteristic of the 'Free Spirit'.

Medieval Women's Mystical Writing

The thirteenth century was an extraordinarily fruitful period for women's mystical writing. New styles were pioneered and existing literary forms remoulded to serve innovatory ends in the creative struggle to express in words the inexpressible experience of God. The adoption of the courtly love lyric for mystical poetry, the presentation of the self and the relationship of the soul to God in autobiographical form, the use of written prose as a literary device, highly charged and erotic images to convey the relationship between Christ and the soul, together with a preference for the vernacular over Latin, are all characteristics common to thirteenth century mystical writings by women.

AUTOBIOGRAPHY AND THE SENSE OF SELF

Women mystics did not write *about God* in any abstract or theorizing sense. Their concern was to document their relationship *with God*. Women's mystical writing is therefore highly personal and, although not autobiographical in the way we understand the term today, is intended to communicate the way in which God has entered and transformed their lives, drawing them into an ever closer perception of the divine presence. Their awareness of the spiritual path made many women highly critical of hypocrisy and corruption among the clergy and impatient of the wealth and self-satisfaction of a Church which often seemed incapable of responding to the needs of the people, needs which their own lives and writings aimed to satisfy.

Although of considerable literary merit, women mystics were not primarily concerned with producing works of literature, however cathartic or creative the process of literary composition may have been. They wrote out of an inner urge to communicate a personal event of great importance. The impulse to write was invariably preceded by a vision, or visions, through which the mystic came to see herself as someone in direct relationship with God. It was her reputation as a visionary which validated the woman mystic's written work, enabling her to communicate other aspects of her experience with equal assurance.

The claim that they were compelled to write by God, and not through any presumption on their part, recurs frequently in women's writing. Lacking the authority of formal theological education, clerical orders or male gender, the only justification for writing was that of being an instrument of the Creator. Hildegard of Bingen describes how she was commanded to write by a heavenly voice, and did so despite her own lack of education, incapacity and the fact that she was a 'mere woman'.[60] Marguerite Porete justified the writing of her *Mirror for Simple Souls* by her identity as 'a creature of God', but nevertheless felt the need to cite three male authorities who had pronounced her book to be inspired by the Holy Spirit, in accordance with the Scriptures and suitable for publication – precautions which did not save her from the inquisitors.

MYSTICAL WRITING AND THE LYRIC OF COURTLY LOVE

The notion of courtly love, and the lyric poetry which it inspired, evolved among the aristocracy of southern France during the twelfth century. Feudal marriages were about property and inheritance, not love, leading to the conviction that true romantic love was only possible outside marriage between a knight and his lady where it could be freely given and received. Although the mannerisms associated with courtly love were limited to a small social group and area, the poetry inspired by the tradition was carried throughout Western Europe, by the troubadours in France, the *Minnesänger* in Germany and proponents of the *dolce stil nuovo* in Italy. Women mystical writers, educated in the secular love lyrics of their day, took this poetic tradition of human sexual love, and transformed it into an account of the relationship between the soul and God. The poetic form and language of courtly love is apparent in the writings of Hadewijch, Mechthild and Beatrice, and their knowledge of secular poetic styles is frequently cited as evidence that they were nobly born.

SANCTITY AND WOMEN'S WRITING

Some of the characteristic elements of women's autobiographical writing, and of the hagiographical *vitae* of women by male chroniclers, can be better understood in the context of the expectations of their audience. The extreme asceticism of Marie of Oignies or Beatrice of Nazareth acted as a recommendation to the ordinary folk that they were especially chosen by God. In *vitae* written soon after the subject's death, miraculous cures and tales of heroic virtues were emphasized so as to convince both ordinary people and the Church authorities that the visionary could intercede for them in heaven and was a suitable candidate for beatification.[61]

The women discussed in this anthology are conforming to the stereotype of the late medieval holy woman in their emphasis on the struggles and hardships that must be endured along the way of sanctity. The journey may be perceived as hard, and love as an illusive goal, but it is a way freely chosen and rewarding in this life, not merely in the life to come. As Hadewijch attests in one of her most beautiful poems:

> If for love you wish to trust yourself to God
> And keep yourself in charity
> Then all shall be yours:
> And you shall win your love.[62]

Notes

1. Power (1987), p. 9.
2. For a fuller discussion of the idea of hierarchy and power see Erler and Kowaleski (1988), pp. 1–17.
3. 'Sententiarum Libri Quatuor' in *Petri Lombardi Opera Omnia*, t. II, quoted in Power (1987), p. 34.
4. Howell (1988), p. 37.
5. Ferrante (1975), p. 6.
6. Quoted in Southern (1970), p. 311. According to Odo, the second abbot of Cluny, 'the highest virtue in a woman is not to wish to be seen', quoted in Schulenburg (1988), p. 117. For a commendably readable account of the development of Western monasticism see Lawrence (1985). See Lucas (1988) and Schulenburg (1988) for an account of early medieval abbesses.
7. Quoted in Bolton (1983), p. 64.
8. Quoted in McDonnell (1954), p. 122.
9. The Apostles were an ascetic body who flourished in the twelfth century around Cologne and at Périgueux in France. They rejected marriage, oath taking and the eating of meat.
10. The term 'Humiliati' came from the description of their clothes as being *'panno humiliti non tincto'*, i.e. simple undyed cloth.
11. They were often referred to simply as *mulieres sanctae*, 'holy women'.
12. McDonnell (1954), p. 73.
13. Quoted in Bolton (1983), p. 87.
14. Rörig (1967), pp. 112–13, notes that few Flemish towns in the later Middle Ages had populations of over 10,000.
15. McDonnell (1954), p. 46.
16. The priory of St Nicholas was founded by a priest, Gilles of Walcourt (d. 1233), and two of his brothers towards the end of the twelfth century. They were not affiliated to any congregation but followed the Rule of St Augustine under the direction of a prior elected by the brethren (see McDonnell (1954), pp. 8–9).
17. See Jacques of Vitry's 'Life' of Marie of Oignies in *Acta Sanctorum*, vol. IV (1867), and Bolton (1983), pp. 88–9.
18. Quoted in McDonnell (1954), pp. 61–2.
19. Quoted in McDonnell (1954), p. 60.
20. Quoted in McDonnell, (1954), p. 6.
21. Matthew Paris, *Chronica Majora* IV, 278, quoted in Southern (1970), p. 319. This account of the beguines was written in 1243.
22. Quoted in Southern (1970), p. 320.
23. Rörig (1967), pp. 116, 122.

24. McDonnell (1954), p. 479.
25. Olyslager (1983), p. 19.
26. Colledge (1965), p. 8.
27. 'Of the hundred and sixty-seven individual beguines whose exact address in Cologne is known between 1263 and 1389, a hundred and thirty-six lived in the neighbourhood of the Dominicans and Franciscans.' Southern (1970), pp. 327–8.
28. Southern (1970), pp. 323–5.
29. Southern (1970), p. 326.
30. Olyslager (1983), pp. 26–7, 135–6.
31. Wilson (1988), traces the history of stigmatism, and suggests a portrait of the personality type associated with this and other related phenomena.
32. *Vita Beatricis*, Prologue, bk. 2, pp. 105–7, 126–7; bk. 3, p. 133, quoted in Bynum (1987a).
33. McDonnell (1954), p. 399.
34. McDonnell (1954), p. 445.
35. Petroff (1986), p. 39.
36. Jacques of Vitry's 'Life' of Marie of Oignies, in Petroff (1986), p. 7.
37. Menzies (1953), p. 98.
38. Quoted in Petroff (1986), pp. 9–10.
39. See *Vita Beatricis*, bk. 3, pp. 180–3, quoted in Bynum (1987a), p. 101.
40. Hart (1980), p. 49.
41. Bynum (1987), pp. 129–30.
42. Weinstein and Bell (1987), quoted in Bynum (1987a), p. 130.
43. Bynum (1987a), p. 131.
44. Bynum (1987a), p. 131.
45. Aleydis is mentioned in Hadewijch's 'List of the Perfect', a supplement to her book of visions which gives the names of the saints she most admired and about eighty living persons known to her. She implies that Aleydis was innocent of the charge of heresy.
46. Gosuin of Bossut, *Vita Idae Nivellensis*, 32, in Chrysostom Henriquez, *Quinque Prudentes Virgines*, Antwerp, 1630, pp. 284–5. Quoted in Hart (1980), p. 4.
47. Lambert (1977), p. 173. For an extremely interesting and detailed account of the question of heresy among the beguines and beghards, see Lerner (1972).
48. Lambert (1977), p. xii.
49. From *Conciliorum Oecumenicorum Decreta*, ed. J. Alberigo, p. 320, quoted in Southern (1970), p. 330.
50. Quoted in Southern (1970), p. 330.

51. Southern (1970), pp. 330–1. Following the Council of Vienne many beghards adopted a Reform and were approved in 1321 by John XXII. They survived until the French Revolution.
52. Quoted in Southern (1970), p. 331.
53. Quoted in Southern (1970), p. 329. In the case of the beghards too enthusiastic an espousal of the *vita apostolica* was often the nub of accusations against them.
54. The term 'beghard' was used by Henry Virneburg, Archbishop of Cologne, to refer to both beguines and beghards.
55. Porete (1981), p. 152.
56. Meister Eckhart was condemned for similar apophatic teaching on the annihilation of the soul in God. Immediately after Marguerite's death Eckhart spent two years in the same Dominican community as her inquisitor, William Humbert, in Paris and would have had ample opportunity to read her work (see Colledge and Marler (1984), p. 15).
57. Lambert (1977), pp. 177–8. See also Labarge (1987), p. 209.
58. Lambert, pp. 177–8.
59. Armstrong (1986), p. 25.
60. Hildegard of Bingen, *Scivias*. For English translations see Francisca Maria Steele, (*The Life and Visions of St. Hildegard*, London, 1914, and Bruce Hozeski, (*Hildegard of Bingen's Scivias*), Santa Fe, 1986.
61. Kieckhefer (1984), pp. 4–5.
62. *Poems in couplets* 6 (see below, p. 99).

PART 2

Selections

I beg you, those who read these words, try to understand them inwardly, in the innermost depths of your understanding, with all the subtle power at your command, or else you run the risk of failing to understand them at all.

Marguerite Porete, *A Mirror for Simple Souls*, p. 27

TRANSLATOR'S NOTE

Throughout the present anthology I have endeavoured to provide translations which reflect the considerable, and at times supremely, poetic quality of the original texts, rather than simply aiming to produce a literal, prose rendering (which though edifying would miss the point). I have also opted for a wholly modern idiom. These writers stood at the very dawn of European vernacular literature, and their revolutionary freshness would be entirely lost by rendering their work into a conventional form of mock-nineteenth century prose.

The name of Mechthild presents fewer problems of pronunciation to the English ear that Hadewijch and Beatrijs (to give her her proper name, although we have used the more familiar Beatrice). Hadewijch was pronounced 'Had – e – week' in Middle Flemish.

The translations of Mechthild are taken from Morel (see Bibliography for details) and Schmidt, who goes back to additional sources for her important Modern German edition. The translations of Beatrice are based on Reypens and Van Mierlo (1926) and Vekeman and Tersteeg (1970), and the references are to the line numbering of the latter text. The translations of Hadewijch are from Van Mierlo (1942, 1947 and 1952).

Mechthild of Magdeburg

All too often the scant knowledge we possess even of major figures in the Middle Ages frustrates our natural desire to know in detail the life circumstances and the personalities of those whose works have become classics of the spiritual life. What we know of Mechthild, for instance, is primarily what she herself tells us in *The Flowing Light of the Godhead* and what we can glean indirectly from that work. She was born around the year 1212 in the diocese of Magdeburg (East Germany). Her familiarity with the *Minnesang*, the German chivalric tradition of 'courtly love', which is evident in the imagery and style of her work suggests that she may have been from a noble background; a view which is supported by the tradition attested in one source that her younger brother was well-educated and became sub-Prior at the Dominican Priory of Halle.

Mechthild herself left her home for Magdeburg in 1230, where she joined a community of beguines. We possess no direct knowledge about the forty years or so which she spent as a beguine, and must rely upon more general information on the beguines in order to fill in this period of her life. We have no firm idea either as to why she sought and gained entrance to the Cistercian convent of Helfta around the year 1270, when she was already an old woman, although this may well have had something to do with the persistent opposition which she seems to have encountered from church authorities during the course of her life. Helfta was a remarkable centre of learning which had developed under the inspiring leadership of Gertrude of Hackeborn, who, from the year 1251 had been abbess of the community. When Mechthild came to Helfta, Gertrude of Hackeborn was still abbess and her sister, Mechthild of Hackeborn, was mistress of the novices. In addition, Gertrude the Great, who was to be much influenced in her own work by the older Mechthild, was a child oblate of the convent. In this centre, women were able to pursue extensive studies and to develop themselves in accordance with a wealth of biblical, patristic and contemporary learning.

It was at the age of twelve, Mechthild tells us, that she first experienced the visions which were to prove such a dominant part of her life. We do not know when she first came to write them down, but we are told that it was at the instigation of her Dominican confessor, Heinrich of Halle, who appears to have encouraged her in her task. The chronology of the seven 'books' which make up *The Flowing Light of the Godhead* cannot be established, but on internal evidence we know that Book Five was completed before 1260 and Book Six by 1271. Book Seven was written in Helfta during the final period of Mechthild's life, and it was there, around the year 1282, that she died.

The history of the transmission of the text of her work has proved particularly complex. It appears that Mechthild herself wrote a series of passages which may then have been collected by her Dominican confessor, Heinrich of Halle, into a single book. This original version of *The Flowing Light of the Godhead* was written in her own Low German dialect, and it has not survived. The text has come down to us principally in two versions. The first of these is a translation which Heinrich of Nordlingen made into Alemannic, which is a more standard dialect of Middle High German, between the years 1343 and 1345.[1] This translation however is not believed to have been made directly from the original, but from some later version. The second text which has survived is a Latin translation which was done shortly after Mechthild's death, around 1285, and which does not include the final Book Seven of her Helfta years. It is also thought that this Latin version imposed its own order upon the original, so it may not be as valuable as the later Alemannic translation.

The work of Mechthild possesses a quite exceptional degree of poetic sensibility in conjunction with a profound and mature faith. Her work is suffused with the warm glow of a personal encounter of love, often expressed through the amorous imagery of the courtly love lyric. Yet this love which Mechthild so sensitively explores has real spiritual depth; she knows of the 'true wilderness', of the sacrifices and hardships which love demands, and of the necessary relinquishing of worldly consolations and values. Mechthild's intense inner life of spiritual encounter finds expression above all in her imagery of 'flowing' and of 'fusion'. This springs from the heart of her unitive experience, and it points to the depths of the mystical interchange of possessing and being possessed by God, her Beloved.

Note

1. See Hans Neumann, 'Beitrage zur Textegeschichte des "Fliessen-den Lichts der Gottheit" und zur Lebensgeschichte Mechthilds von Magdeburg' (*Nachrichten der Akademie der Wissenschaften in Göttingen*, Göttingen 1954, pp. 27–80) for a detailed account of the transmission of the text.

The content of this book is seen, heard and felt in all my members

Neither can I write nor do I wish to write unless I first see with the eyes of my soul and hear with the ears of my eternal spirit and sense in all the members of my body the power of the Holy Spirit.

4:13

The conversation of love and the queen

The soul drew close to love,
Greeted her reverently
And said: God greet you, Lady Love!

LOVE: May God reward you, dear Queen.

SOUL: Lady Love, you are most perfect.

LOVE: O Queen, that is why I rule all things . . .

SOUL: Lady Love, you have taken from me all that I ever possessed on earth.

LOVE: But Lady Queen, what a blessed exchange!

SOUL: Lady Love, you took from me my childhood.

LOVE: Lady Queen, in return I give you heavenly freedom.

SOUL: Lady Love, you took from me all my youth.

LOVE: Lady Queen, in return I gave you many holy virtues.

SOUL: Lady Love, you took from me my family and my friends.

LOVE: O dear! What a pitiful lament, Lady Queen.

SOUL: Lady Love, you took from me worldly honours, worldly wealth and the whole world.

LOVE: Lady Queen, I shall make good your loss with the Holy Spirit in a single hour, according to your wish.

SOUL: Lady Love, you overwhelmed me so completely that my body writhed in a strange sickness.

LOVE: Lady Queen, in return I gave you sublime knowledge and profound thoughts.

SOUL: Lady Love, you have consumed all my flesh and blood.

LOVE: Lady Queen, you have been purified and drawn up to God.

SOUL: Lady Love, you are a thief; you must give me yet more in return.

LOVE: Lady Queen, then take me myself!

SOUL: Lady Love, now you have repaid me with a hundred-fold on earth.

LOVE: Lady Queen, now you may ask that God and all His riches be given you.

1:1

How the soul speaks to God

Lord, you are my lover,
My longing,
My flowing stream,
My sun,
And I am your reflection.

1:4

How God answers the soul

It is my nature that makes me love you often,
For I am love itself.

It is my longing that makes me love you intensely,
For I yearn to be loved from the heart.

It is my eternity that makes me love you long,
For I have no end.

1:24

You should ask God to love you long, often and intensely so that you may be pure, beautiful and holy

O Lord,
Love me intensely,
Love me often and long!
For the more often you love me, the purer I become.
The more intensely you love me, the more beautiful I
 become.
The longer you love me, the holier I become.

1:23

How God comes to the soul

I descend on my love
As dew on a flower.

1:13

On knowledge and delight

Love without knowledge
For the wise soul is darkness,
Knowledge without delight
Seems to her the pain of hell,
But delight without death
She laments without end.

1:21

On the way of suffering for God joyfully

God leads his chosen children
Along strange paths.
And it is a strange path,
And a noble path,
And a holy path
Which God himself walked:
To suffer pain without sin or guilt.
But this gives delight to the soul
Who desires God.

1:25

The way along which the soul draws the senses and thus becomes free from grief

It is a rare
And a high way,
Which the soul follows,
Drawing the senses after,
Just as the person with sight leads the blind.
In this way the soul is free
And lives without the heart's grief,
Desiring nothing but her Lord,
Who works all things well.

1:26

In suffering you should be a lamb, a turtledove and a bride

You are my lamb in your suffering.
You are my turtledove in your sighing.
You are my bride in your waiting.

1:34

The wilderness has twelve things

You should love what is not
And flee what is.
You should stand alone
And approach no one.
You should strive always
To be free from all things.
You should free the bound
And bind the free.
You should comfort the sick
And yet possess nothing.
You should drink the water of suffering
And feed the fire of love with the fuel of virtue.
Then you shall live in the true wilderness.

1:35

On sevenfold perfection

The soul that thirsts for God willingly renounces empty fame and is:

> willingly without honour
> willingly disregarded
> willingly alone
> willingly still
> willingly lowly
> willingly raised up
> willingly united.

2:12

On the seven gifts of a brother

His soul is groundless in desire,
Burning in love,
Kind in his presence,
A mirror of the world,
Humble in his greatness,
True in his help,
Gathered in God.

2:16

How God woos the soul and makes it wise in his love

Thus God frees the simple soul and makes it wise in his love:

> Oh precious dove,
> Your feet are red,
> Your feathers smooth,
> Your mouth well-formed,
> Your eyes beautiful,
> Your head noble,
> Your movements delightful,
> Your flight is swift and bold,
> Too soon you return to earth.

2:17

On the seven sins

Lack of virtue is a very harmful quality in us.
Bad habits harm us in every way.
Earthly desire kills in us the word of God.
Wilful obstinacy wreaks much havoc in us.
Enmity of heart drives out the Holy Spirit.
An angry heart robs us of God's intimacy.
False piety can never endure,
But the true love of God shall never pass.
And if we do not flee these enemies,
Then they shall steal Paradise from us.
For we make a heaven on earth
When we lead a holy life here below.

3:7

How a free soul speaks to God with love

Lord, because I am beneath all creatures, you have raised me up above all things to yourself. And, Lord, because I have no earthly treasure, neither do I have an earthly heart. Since you, Lord, are my treasure, you are also my heart and my sole good.

4:7

How the bride who is united with God spurns the consolation of all creatures

I cannot endure a single consolation
But my beloved.
I love my earthly friends
As companions in eternity
And I love my enemies
With a painful and holy longing
For their blessedness.
In all things God has a sufficiency
But in the touching of my soul.

4:12

God's absence

Ah blessed absence of God,
How lovingly I am bound to you!
You strengthen my will in its pain
And make dear to me the long, hard wait in my poor body.
The nearer I come to you,
The more wonderfully and abundantly God comes upon
   me.
In pride, alas, I can easily lose you,
But in the depths of pure humility, O Lord,
I cannot fall away from you.

For the deeper I fall,
The sweeter you taste.

4:12

The power of love

Love penetrates the senses and storms the soul with all its power. When love grows in the soul, then it rises up with great longing to God and flowingly expands to receive the miracle that breaks in upon it. Love melts through the soul and into the senses. And so the body too gains its part and conforms in all ways to love.

5:4

Four kinds of humility

The first form of humility can be seen in the clothes that we wear, which should be of an appropriate style and clean, and in the place where we live. The second is apparent in the way that we behave towards others, whether we are loving in all circumstances and in all things. This causes the love of God to grow. The third kind of humility appears in the senses and in the way that we use and love all things rightly. The fourth form of humility lives in the soul, which is the self-effacing humility which creates so much sweet wonder in the loving soul. And it is this humility which makes us rise up to Heaven . . .

5:4

How sin is like the greatness of God

Nothing is as great as the greatness of my God but the
greatness of my sin.

5:10

On the tenfold value of the prayer of a good person

The prayer has great power
Which we pray with all our strength.
It makes an embittered heart mellow,
A sad heart joyful,
A foolish heart wise,
A timid heart bold,
A weak heart strong,
A blind heart clear-seeing,
A cold heart ardent.
It draws God who is great into a heart which is small.
It drives the hungry soul up to the fullness of God.
It unites the two lovers, God and soul, in a place of bliss,
Where they converse long of love.

5:13

The love of God

Ah, dear love of God, always embrace this soul of mine,
For it pains me above all things
When I am separated from you.
Ah, love, do not allow me to grow cool
For all my works are dead
When I can feel you no longer.
O love, you sweeten both suffering and need;
You teach and console the true children of God.

5:30

Lady love

O lady love, cast me beneath your feet!
I delight when victorious you vanquish me
And through you my life is destroyed
For in that, O lady, lies my true safety.

5:30

The song of love

O sweet love of God, when I sleep too long,
Unmindful of things that are good,
Then, please, wake me up and sing
For me, O lady, your song
With which you touch my soul
As if with the sweet sound of strings.

5:30

How you should behave in fourteen things

When you pray, you should make yourself small in great
humility,

When you confess your sins, you should do so frankly,

When you perform penances, you should do so with
commitment,

When you eat, you should be restrained,

When you sleep, you should do so in an orderly way,

When you are alone, you should be faithful,

When you are in company, you should be wise,

When someone teaches you good habits, you should be
attentive,

When someone rebukes you, you should be patient,

When you do something good, then you should regard
yourself as poor,

When you do something that is wrong, then you should
immediately seek grace,

When you are being vain, then you should feel fear,

When you are troubled, then you should have great trust in
God,

When you work with your hands, you should do so
swiftly,

So you can banish evil thoughts.

6:12

Temptation, the world and a good end test us

We do not know how firmly we stand
until we feel the temptation of the body.

We do not know how strong we are
until the evil of the world attacks us.

We do not know what goodness there is in us,
until we die a holy death.

6:40

The will of God

The greatest joy in heaven is the will of God. When self-will turns to his will, then divine joy enters the troubled heart of men and women. This is the confession of a spiritual person, that they have neglected the gift which comes from God.

We should receive painful gifts with joy, consoling gifts with fear; and then we shall be able to make use of all things which befall us. Dear friend, be one with God and delight in his will.

6:42

God speaks to the soul

And God said to the soul:
    I desired you before the world began.
    I desire you now
    As you desire me.
    And where the desires of two come together
    There love is perfected.

7:16

The loving soul speaks to her Lord

If the whole world belonged to me alone,
And if it were all of pure gold
And if I could reign eternally here
The noblest, finest and richest queen
According to my wish,
Then still I would regard it as folly
For I am far too fond of looking upon
Jesus Christ, my dear Lord,
In his heavenly honour.
Just look and see how they suffer
Who have lived long without him.

7:40

How we should prepare ourselves for God

When a bird rests long on the ground, then its wings become weak and its feathers grow heavy. Then it stretches upwards, ruffles its plumage and strains upwards towards the heavens until it feels the air and takes flight. The longer it flies, the more blissfully it soars, and scarcely returns to earth for its nourishment. For the wings of love have quite removed its earthly desire. In the same way we should prepare to rise up on high. We should constantly turn the feathers of our longing towards God. We should rise up in the virtues and good works of love. And if we do not cease in our striving, then we will know God.

7:61

How God adorns the soul with its sufferings

We wear our everyday work clothes when we are healthy
And, when we are ill, our bridal dress.

7:65

How you should give thanks and pray

Lord, Father, I thank you for creating me,
Lord, Jesus Christ, I thank you for being my salvation,
Lord, Holy Spirit, I thank you for purifying me,
Lord, one and undivided Trinity, I pray to you
That now, mindful of all faithfulness,
You grant me a merciful death
To release me from my suffering:
In manus tuas commendo spiritum meum

6:27

Beatrice of Nazareth

Beatrice was born around the year 1200, and was probably the youngest child of a well-established merchant family from Tienen in the Belgian Brabant. On the death of her mother at the age of seven Beatrice was sent by her father, Barthelmy de Vleeschouwer, to study with the beguines at Zoutleeuw (Léau), although he later sent her to continue her studies at the Cistercian convent of Bloemendael (Florival) which he had himself recently founded. In 1215 Beatrice was clothed as a Cistercian nun together with her sisters Christina and Sybilla. Before her next move, in 1221, to the new foundation of Maagdendael near Oplinter, Beatrice spent several months in the Abbey La Ramée near Nivelles where she trained in the illumination of manuscripts. It was during this period that she met the visionary and mystical writer Iva of Nivelles, who was to become a close friend. Again with her sisters, Beatrice finally moved, in around 1250, to the convent of Our Lady of Nazareth at Lier, near Antwerp, founded by her father at Beatrice's request, where she lived as prioress until her death in 1268.

Beatrice wrote numerous works during her lifetime, the only one of which to survive in her original Flemish is the *Seven Degrees of Love*. Most of her lost compositions are allegorical works on the spiritual life. There is evidence that Beatrice kept her own diary, and the notes she wrote for her own autobiography formed the basis for her *vita*, which was written by an unknown hand. The *Seven Degrees of Love*, originally a part of her autobiography, is the first work, written in a vernacular tongue to explore the ascent of the soul to God.

The influence of Bernard of Clairvaux may be detected in Beatrice's *Seven Degrees of Love* and, as in Mechthild, there is evidence of her familiarity with the imagery of courtly love. With Beatrice the poetic feel, so exquisitely present in Mechthild, is submerged beneath the energy of her visionary ascent from 'lower' forms of love to the highest love of all, in which we both 'die' and 'live', and in which we gain an ecstatic foretaste of the bliss of Heaven.

Love's striving

In all that she does, love strives only for the purity, the nobility and the highest excellence which she herself is, which she possesses and enjoys within herself, and it is this same striving which love teaches to those who seek to follow her.

71–75

Love without return

And there is another manner of loving, which is when the soul seeks to serve our Lord for nothing in return, for love alone, without demanding to know the reason why and without any reward of grace or glory; just as the lady serves her lord for the sake of her love without any thought of reward, for whom simply to serve him is enough and that he should allow her to serve him. In the same way she desires to serve love with love beyond measure and beyond all human reason with all her deeds of fidelity.

And when this comes upon her, then she is so consumed with desire, so ready to perform any service, so cheerful in toil, so gentle in tribulation, so light-hearted in sadness, and she desires with all her being to serve him. And so it is her delight when she finds something she can do or endure in the service of love and in its honour.

76–99

The power of love

Sometimes it happens that love is sweetly awoken in the soul and joyfully arises and moves in the heart of itself without us doing anything at all. And then the heart is so powerfully touched by love, so keenly drawn into love and so strongly seized by love, and so utterly mastered by love and so tenderly embraced by love that it entirely yields itself to love. And in this it experiences a great proximity to God, a spiritual radiance, a marvellous bliss, a noble freedom, an ecstatic sweetness, a great overpowering by the strength of love, and an overflowing abundance of immense delight. And then she feels that all her senses are sanctified by love and her will has become love, and that she is so deeply immersed and so engulfed in the abyss of love that she herself has turned entirely into love. Then the beauty of love has bedecked her, the power of love has devoured her, the sweetness of love has submerged her, the grandeur of love has consumed her, the nobility of love has enveloped her, the purity of love has adorned her, and the sublimity of love has drawn her upwards and so united herself with her that she always must be love and do nothing but the deeds of love.

170–206

The goad of love

For the more the soul is given from above, the more she desires, and the more that is revealed to her, the more she is seized by a desire to draw near to the light of truth, of purity, of sanctity and of love's delight. And thus she is driven and goaded on more and more and knows no peace or satisfaction; for the very thing that tortures her and gives her the greatest suffering, makes her whole, and what wounds her most deeply, is the source of her greatest relief.

300–310

The immensity of love

And so as the fish swims in the vastness of the oceans and rests in the deeps, and as the bird boldly soars in the heights and the vastness of the air, in the same way she feels her spirit roam free through the depths and the heights and the immensity of love.

347–354

The faithfulness of love

All those who want to attain to love must seek it with fear and pursue it with constant faithfulness, exercising an intense longing and willingly suffering without any hesitation great burdens, much pain and tribulation. They must consider every small thing to be great until they have progressed so far along the path that love reigns in them, and perfects in them her mighty works, making all things seem small, easing our toil, soothing our pain and wiping away all the debts we owe her.

This is freedom of conscience and sweetness of heart. It is docility of mind, nobility of soul, sublimity of spirit and the beginning of eternal life. This is to live even on earth the life of angels which is followed by life eternal which, we pray, God in his goodness shall grant us all.

371–392

The eternity of love

But the blessed soul has a further manner of sublime loving which moves it greatly from within. This is when it is drawn up above human things in love, above human thinking and reason and above all the works of the heart and is drawn by eternal love alone into the eternity of love, into the incomprehensible breadth, the unattainable heights and the immense abyss of the Godhead, which is all in all things and which is immutably all-existent, all-mighty, all-comprehending and all-powerful in its deeds.

394–409

The desire for God

The soul seeks God in his majesty; she follows him there and gazes upon him with heart and spirit. She knows him, she loves him and she so burns with desire for him that she cannot pay heed to any saints or sinners, angels or creatures, except with that all-comprehending love of him by whom she loves all things. She has chosen him alone in love above all, beneath all and within all, and so she desires to see God, to possess and to enjoy him with all the longing of her heart and with all the strength of her soul.

446–458

The vision of love

Therefore the soul always wills to follow love, to know love and to delight in love. But she cannot do so in this exile. And so she desires to return to her homeland where she has already made her dwelling and to which she turns with all her will and where she will finally rest in love. For this she knows well: there, all obstacles will be removed from her and she will be received in love by Love.

And there she will eagerly look upon him whom she has loved so tenderly and shall possess him for her eternal good whom she has so faithfully served. And she will enjoy him in the fullness of delight whom she has embraced so often in her soul with love . . .

There the soul is united with her bridegroom and becomes one spirit with him in indivisible love and eternal fidelity. And the soul who strove her utmost in the time of grace shall savour him in everlasting glory, when praise and love shall be all our work.

552–581

Hadewijch of Brabant

We know very little about the author of these works, apart from what we can deduce from the writings themselves. Hadewijch was a common name and has defied precise identification. It appears that Hadewijch was a beguine, probably the mistress of a beguine convent. She evidently received much criticism and opposition and, for reasons which are unclear, may have been forced to leave the beguines with whom she lived. She continued to write to the young beguines who had been her charges and admonished them to remain true to the path they had chosen, being prepared to give up everything for the love of God.

Hadewijch knew French and Latin, which fact together with her use of chivalric motifs argues strongly for an aristocratic upbringing. She writes in the dialect of medieval Brabant and most probably came from the area around Antwerp or Brussels. Her works are dated to around the first half of the thirteenth century (*c.* 1221–40).

The heart of Hadewijch's work is a mysticism of love, and it is this which in different forms finds expression throughout her letters, visions and poems. The influences upon her, as upon Beatrice, who has a number of images in common with Hadewijch, are certainly those other writers of a love-based mysticism, including William of Saint Thierry, who came originally from Liège, and Bernard of Clairvaux. Although the work of Hadewijch and Beatrice owes a debt to these writers, it is never merely derivative and represents an experiential radicalization of the theology of love. For Hadewijch, Love (*Minne*) becomes her spouse, her Lady mistress, her God, her companion, a mistress who leads Hadewijch through bleak times, moments of isolation and despair, as well as giving her periods of rapture and delight. In her visions, Hadewijch is led to a knowledge of the mysteries of heaven, and is reassured that her present sufferings are temporary, a sign of God's preferential love.

The works of Hadewijch, which include letters, poems in stanzas, poems in couplets (excluding numbers 17–29 which are by another hand) and visions were soon lost to view until their rediscovery in the nineteenth century. They were read in the fourteenth century, however, by the great Flemish mystic, Jan van Ruusbroec (1293–1381), who found in both Hadewijch and Beatrice much inspiration. Ruusbroec's themes of the primacy of love, his images of the 'storm', the 'fury' and the 'delight' of love, as well as his idea of 'living in the Trinity', are all things which he has in common with the earlier Brabantine tradition of these women mystics.

Suffering for love

If you want to come to the highest love
And follow her way in perfection
Then you should always seek with a burning heart
New sufferings for love.
You should allow love herself to act,
For she will make good all your pain with love.
And if you do not suffer her pain
Then you do not love her, that much is clear . . .
So desire suffering in order to ascend on high
And that united in one knowledge
We may together delight in our love.
Now let us both adorn ourselves
So that love herself may lead us
To the blissful place love has prepared
Where she shall dwell eternally.

Poems in Couplets 5

Winning love

O love, set your whole mind
On God's love who made you.
Commit all your being to love;
And then you shall heal all your wounds,
Neither fearing pain nor
Fleeing from sorrow in anything.
You should rely on love
And then you shall know what to love and what to hate.
Be content with all things:
For that is the sign of love's presence,
And that you are so easily oppressed
Denies you many a beautiful gift.
If for love you wish to trust yourself to God
And keep yourself in charity
Then all shall be yours:
And you shall win your love.

Poems in Couplets 6

On discernment

Note whether what enters your mind
Does you harm or good,
Whether it is of the spirit or the will;
There lies the greatest discernment of all.
People think that they are led by the Spirit,
When mostly it is their own will that leads them,
And they regard as consolation from God
What leads them to their doom.

Poems in Couplets 11

The paradoxes of love

The storming of love is what is sweetest within her,
Her deepest abyss is her most beautiful form,
To lose our way in her is to arrive,
To hunger for her is to feed and to taste,
Her despairing is sureness of faith,
Her worst wounding is to become whole again,
To waste away for her is to endure,
Her hiding is to find her at all times,
To be tormented for her is to be in good health,
In her concealment she is revealed,
What she withholds, she gives,
Her finest speech is without words,
Her imprisonment is freedom,
Her most painful blow is her sweetest consolation,
Her giving is her taking away,
Her going away is her coming near,
Her deepest silence is her highest song,
Her greatest wrath is her warmest thanks,
Her greatest threatening is remaining true,
Her sadness is the healing of all sorrow.

Poems in Couplets 13

The fury of love

I greet what I love
With my heart's blood
And my senses wither
In love's fury.

Poems in Couplets 15

The sacrifice of true love

For love there is no way forward
But to receive all blows and all consolations,
And we should seek the sacrifice of true love
Within the heart which keeps faith:
If we do thus, then we shall conquer
And, though we are far off, attain knowledge.

Poems in Couplets 16

The humanity of Christ

This is how everyone today loves themselves: they want to live with God in consolation, in wealth and in splendour, and to share in the delight of his glory. We all wish to be God with God. But, God knows, there are few enough of us who want to live as men and women with his humanity or to bear his cross with him, and to be crucified with him in order to pay for the sins of the whole world . . .

Letters 6

To live Christ in his divinity and humanity

You should live on earth with the humanity of God when you experience suffering and troubles, while inwardly loving and rejoicing with the almighty and eternal Godhead in sweet abandonment.

In both these truths there lies a single delight. And just as the humanity of Christ on earth yielded to the will of his majesty, so too you should yield in love to the will of both together. Serve humbly under their one power, standing always before them as one who follows their will in its entirety. And let them do with you whatever they will.

Do not involve yourself with anything else. But serve the humanity with ready and faithful hands and with a will firm in all virtues. And you should not love the Godhead with devotion alone, but also with inexpressible desires, standing always with new zeal before that fearful and marvellous countenance which is Love's revelation of herself.

Letters 6

The service of Love

Before Love breaks through and before she transports us out of ourselves and so touches us with herself that we become one spirit and one being with her and in her, we must first offer her fine service and suffering: fine service in all the works of virtue and suffering in total obedience to her. Thus we must stand with renewed vigour and with hands which are ever ready for virtuous work, and with a will that is ready for all those virtues in which Love in honoured, with no other goal than that Love should take her rightful place among us and in all creatures, according to our debt to her. This is to hang on the cross with Christ, to die with him and to rise again with him. May he always help us to this end.

Letters 6

Enduring all things for Love

Whoever loves is bound to renounce all things and to regard themselves as being the least of all in order to satisfy Love according to her worth. Whoever loves, allows themselves willingly to be corrected, without seeking excuses, in order to be the freer in love. And willingly they will endure much for the sake of Love. Whoever loves suffers blows willingly for their formation. Whoever loves is willingly cast out in order to be wholly free. Whoever loves is willingly alone in order to love Love and to possess her.

Letters 8

Union with God

May God make known to you, dear child, who he is and how he treats his servants and especially his handmaids; how he consumes them within himself. From the depths of his wisdom, he shall teach you what he is and with what wonderful sweetness the one lover lives in the other and so permeates the other that they do not know themselves from each other. But they possess each other in mutual delight, mouth in mouth, heart in heart, body in body, soul in soul, while a single divine nature flows through them both and they both become one through each other, yet remaining always themselves.

Letters 9

Virtue is the measure of love

Whoever loves God, loves his works. Now the works of God are noble virtues. Therefore, whoever loves God, loves virtue. This love is true and full of consolation. It is virtue which proves the presence of love, not sweetness of devotion, for it sometimes happens that those who love less, feel more sweetness. But it is not according to what we feel that love is measured, but according to the extent that we are grounded in charity and rooted in love.

Letters 10

Learning perfection

If you want to know this perfection, then you must first learn to know yourself in all that you do, in what you are willing to do and what you are not willing to do, in what you love and what you hate, in what you trust and what you do not trust, and in all that happens to you. You have to consider by yourself how you endure what opposes you and how you are able to go without those things which are dear to you. Of all the things that can befall a young heart, this is truly the hardest one of all: going without what we like. And when something good befalls you, examine to what use you can put it, and how wise and how moderate you are with regard to it. Try and remain inwardly detached in all that happens to you: when you are troubled or when you enjoy peace of mind. And always contemplate the works of our Lord, for these can teach you perfection.

Letters 14

The deepest essence of the soul

Now understand the deepest essence of the soul: what the soul is. The soul is an essence which is transparent to God and for which God too is transparent. And the soul is more than this: it is an essence which wants to give delight to God, and which preserves its worth as long as it does not fall away to things which are alien to it, and which are unworthy of it. And when the soul preserves its worth, then it becomes a groundless abyss where God is his own delight and in which he for ever takes pleasure in himself in the fullest degree, as the soul does for ever in him. The soul is the way that God goes when he proceeds from his depths to his liberty, and God is the way the soul goes when it too enters its liberty, that is into his ground, which is beyond the reach of all things but the soul's depths. And as long as God is not wholly her own possession, she will not be satisfied.

Letters 18

Love's completeness

Nothing dwells or can dwell in Love, nor can anything touch her except desire. And 'touch' is Love's most secret name, which springs forth from Love herself. For Love is always desiring and touching and consuming within herself. And yet she is complete within herself. Love can dwell in all things. She can dwell in charity, while charity cannot dwell in Love, any more than mercy can, or graciousness, or humility, or reason, or fear, or thrift, or moderation, or anything at all. And yet she can dwell in all these things, which are all sustained by Love. And yet nothing sustains Love herself but her own wholeness.

Letters 20

The temptations of the world

We have too much self-will, we seek too much repose and we are too concerned with our own peace and our ease. We become too easily tired, depressed and dejected. We are not prepared to endure any setback. We are too keen to know what we lack, and then we are over-concerned with getting hold of it instead of enduring this privation. It offends us when someone attacks us or calls our experience of God into doubt or robs us of our peace, our honour, or our friends. We wish to be godly in church but at home and elsewhere we wish to know about all those worldly things that help us or harm us. There we find the time to be with our friends, to talk and to socialize, to quarrel and to make up. We wish to win for ourselves a good name by small acts of love and we get excited about nice clothes, about fine food, things of beauty and the unnecessary pleasures of the world. For no one should use entertainments in order to escape from God. For he always comes with new power . . . For it is we who fall from God, not God from us. And since we withhold things from Love, we do not wear her crown and are not exalted or honoured by her.

Because of this we are hindered in all respects, while true Faith and Love remain beyond our reach. And since there are so many faults within us, we remain stunted in the spiritual life and imperfect in all virtues. And for this reason, no one else can help us. O Lord, how difficult it is! God must increase in us and so perfect our being that the Trinity may delight in us and we may become one with the unity of the Godhead.

Letters 30

The freedom of love

Just as the beautiful and dew-covered rose
Rises from among thorns,
So shall they who love stand fast in the storm
In all evils that afflict them, with trust:
Free and without delusion
They shall flourish despite all harm.
Those who lack love
Are soon brought to their knees.
While those who love are free.

Poems in Stanzas 2

The service of Love

We are too half-hearted in the service of Love,
And so we are not her true possession
And remain poor; but all of us should know this:
To the one of whom Love approves,
She gives her kingdom and her treasure.

Poems in Stanzas 3

Following Love

Sometimes gentle and sometimes stern,
Sometimes dark and sometimes bright,
In consolation that sets free
And in fear that constrains,
In receiving and in giving
Those who stray on the paths of Love
Must always live here below.

Poems in Stanzas 5

Works of faithfulness

Some are of the opinion
That their success in love is great
So all the world blooms for them
And turns green.
But then we learn the truth
And see that it is not so:
For it is only our works of faithfulness
That prove our progress in love.

Poems in Stanzas 13

Love's constancy

Anyone who has waded
Through Love's turbulent waters,
Now feeling hunger and now satiety,
Is untouched by the seasons
Of withering or blooming,
For in the deepest
And most dangerous waters,
On the highest peaks,
Love is always the same.

Poems in Stanzas 14

The profit of Love

All that I am
I have given to sublime Love
Whether I win or I lose,
She shall receive all that is hers by right.
But what has happened to me?
I am no longer my own possession,
For she has engulfed my whole being,
And her noble nature convinces me
That all suffering for Love is profit.

Poems in Stanzas 16

Love's maturity

In the beginning Love satisfies us,
When Love first spoke to me of love –
How I laughed at her in return!
But then she made me like the hazel trees,
Which blossom early in the season of darkness,
And bear fruit slowly.

Poems in Stanzas 17

Knowing Love in herself

I do not complain of suffering for Love,
It is right that I should always obey her,
For I can know her only as she is in herself,
Whether she commands in storm or in stillness.
This is a marvel beyond my understanding,
Which fills my whole heart
And makes me stray in a wild desert.

Poems in Stanzas 22

The madness of love

The madness of love
Is a blessed fate;
And if we understood this
We would seek no other:
It brings into unity
What was divided,
And this is the truth:
Bitterness it makes sweet,
It makes the stranger a neighbour,
And what was lowly it raises on high.

Poems in Stanzas 28

Drawing close to Love

I drew so close to Love
That I began to understand
How great the gain of those
Who give themselves wholly to Love:
And when I saw this for myself,
What was lacking in me gave me pain.

Poems in Stanzas 30

The power of Love

Since I gave myself to the service of Love,
Winning or losing,
I am resolved:
I shall give her thanks at all times,
Winning or losing,
I shall live under her power.

Poems in Stanzas 30

Mary, Mother of Love

Whatever gifts God bestowed upon us
There was no one who could
Understand true love
Until Mary, in her goodness,
And with deep humility,
Received the gift of Love,
She it was who tamed wild Love
And gave us a lamb for a lion;
Through her a light shone in the darkness
That had endured so long.

Poems in Stanzas 29

Select Bibliography

TEXTS

Mechthild of Magdeburg

Menzies, L., *The Revelations of Mechthild of Magdeburg (1210–1297) or The Flowing Light of the Godhead*. London, Longman, Green and Co. 1953. Complete English translation.

Morel, G. P., ed., *Offenbarungen oder Das Fleissende Licht der Gottheit*. Regensburg 1869, reprinted Darmstadt 1963, 1976.

Schmidt, M., ed., *Mechthild von Magdeburg: Das Fleissende Licht der Gottheit*. Benziger Verlag, Einsiedeln 1955. Modern German edition.

Beatrice of Nazareth

Colledge, E., *Medieval Netherlands Religious Literature*. Leiden and New York 1965. Complete English translation of *The Seven Manners of Loving*.

Reypens, L., ed., *De Autobiographie van de z. Beatrijs van Tienen*. Antwerp 1964.

Reypens, L., and van Mierlo, J., eds., *Seven Manieren van Minne*. Leuven, 1926.

Vekeman, H., and Tersteeg, J., *Beatrijs van Nazareth. Van Seven Manieren van Heiliger Minne*. Zutphen 1970.

Hadewijch of Brabant

Alaerts, J., *De Wetten van de Minne: met de tekst van Hadewijchs 45 Strofische Gedichten volgens HS. 385 II van het Ruusbroecgenootschap*. 2 vols. Bonheiden 1977.

Hart, C., *Hadewijch: The Complete Works*. New York, Paulist Press; London SPCK 1980. Complete English translation.

Mierlo, J. van, ed., *Hadewijch: Strophische Gedichten*. Antwerp 1942.

Mierlo, J. van, ed., *Hadewijch: Brieven*, 2 vols. Antwerp 1947.

Mierlo, J. van, ed., *Hadewijch: Mengeldichten*. Antwerp 1952.

STUDIES

Armstrong, K. (1987) *The Gospel According to Woman*. London, Pan Books.

Asen, J. (1927–8) 'Die Beginen in Köln', *Annalen des Hist. Vereins f. den Niederrhein*, cxi, 81–180; cxii, 71–148; cxiii, 13–96.

Baker, D., ed. (1972) *Schism, Heresy and Religious Protest*. Studies in Church History 9, Cambridge University Press.

Baker, D., ed. (1973) *Sanctity and Secularity: the Church and the World*. Studies in Church History 10, Oxford, Blackwell.

Baker, D., ed. (1978) *Medieval Women*. Studies in Church History, Subsidia I, Oxford, Blackwell.

Bolton, B. (1973) '*Mulieres Sanctae*', in Baker (1973), pp. 77–95.

Bolton, B. (1978) '*Vitae Matrum*: A Further Aspect of the *Frauenfrage*', in Baker (1978), pp. 253–73.

Bolton, B. (1981) '*Vitae Matrum*' and 'Some Thirteenth Century Women in the Low Countries: A Special Case?', *Nederlands Archief voor Kerkgeschiedenis* 61, pp. 7–29.

Bolton, B. (1983) *The Medieval Reformation*. London, Edward Arnold.

Bolton, B. (1985) '*Via Ascetica*: A Papal Quandary', in W. J. Sheils, ed., *The Church and Healing*, Studies in Church History 22, Oxford, Blackwell, pp. 161–91.

Bullough, V. L. (1973) 'Medieval and Scientific View of Women', *Viator* 4, pp. 487–93.

Bynum, C. W. (1982) *Jesus as Mother: Studies in the Spirituality of the High Middle Ages*. Berkeley CA: University of California Press.

Bynum, C. W. (1987a) 'Religious Women in the Later Middle Ages', in Raitt (1987), pp. 121–39.

Bynum, C. W., (1987b) *Holy Feast and Holy Fast: The Religious Significance of Food to Medieval Women*. Berkeley CA, University of California Press.

Colledge, E. (1965). See *Texts* above.

Colledge, E., and Marler, J. C. (1984) 'Poverty of the Will: Ruusbroec, Eckhart and *The Mirror of Simple Souls*', in P. Mommaers and de Paepe, N., eds. *Jan van Ruusbroec: the sources, content and sequels of his mysticism*, Leuven University Press, pp. 14–47.

Davies, O. (1988) *God Within: The Mystical Tradition of Northern Europe*. London, Darton, Longman & Todd.

Dronke, P. (1984) *Women Writers of the Middle Ages: A Critical Study of Texts from Perpetua to Marguerite Porete*. Cambridge University Press.

Erler, M. and Kowaleski, M., eds. (1988) *Women and Power in the Middle Ages*. Athens GA, University of Georgia Press.

Ferrante, J. (1975) *Women as Image in Medieval Literature*. New York, Columbia University Press.

Franklin, J. C. (1978) *Mystical Transformations: The Imagery of Liquids in the Work of Mechthild of Magdeburg*. New Jersey, Cranbury; London, Associated University Presses.

Goodich, M. (1981) 'Contours of Female Piety in Later Medieval Hagiography'; *Church History* 50, pp. 20–32.

Goodich, M. (1982) *Vita Perfect: The Ideal of Sainthood in the Thirteenth Century*. Stuttgart.

Grundmann, H. (1961) *Religiöse Bewegungen im Mittelalter*. Reprint with additions, Hildesheim.

Grundmann, H. (1964) 'Die geschichtliche Grundlagen der deutschen Mystik', in K. Ruh, ed., *Altdeutsche und Altiederländische Mystik*, Darmstadt, pp. 72–99.

Grundmann, H. (1965) 'Ketzerverhöre des Spätmittelaltes als quellenkritisches Problem', *Deutsches Archiv* xxi, pp. 519–75.

Haas, A. M., 'Schools of Late Medieval Mysticism', in Raitt (1987), pp. 140–3.

Hart, C. (1980), see *Texts*, above.

Howell, M. C. (1986) *Women, Production and Patriarchy in Late Medieval Cities*. Chicago IL, University of Chicago Press.

Howell, M. C. (1988) 'Citizenship and Gender: Women's Political Status in Northern Medieval Cities', in Erler and Kowaleski (1988), pp. 37–60.

Kieckhefer, R. (1984) *Unquiet Souls: Fourteenth Century Saints and Their Religious Milieu*. Chicago IL, University of Chicago Press.

Labarge, M. W. (1987) *Women in Medieval Life: A Small Sound of the Trumpet*. London, Hamish Hamilton.

Lagorio, V. M. (1984) 'The Medieval Continental Women Mystics: An Introduction', in P. E. Szarmach, ed., *An Introduction to the Medieval Mystics of Europe*, Albany NY, State University of New York Press, pp. 161–94.

Lambert, M. D. (1977) *Medieval Heresy: Popular Movements from Bogomil to Hus*. London, Edward Arnold.

Lawrence, C. H. (1985) *Medieval Monasticism: Forms of Religious Life in Western Europe in the Middle Ages*. London, Longman.

Lerner, R. E. (1972) *The Heresy of the Free Spirit in the Later Middle Ages*. Berkeley CA, University of California Press.

Lerner, R. E. (1983) 'Beguines and Beghards', in J. Strayer, ed., *Dictionary of the Middle Ages* 2, New York, Scribner, pp. 157–62.

Lucas, A. M. (1988) *Women in the Middle Ages: Religion, Marriage and Letters*. Brighton, Harvester Press.

McDonnell, E. (1954) *The Beguines and Beghards in Medieval Culture*. Brunswick NJ, Rutgers University Press.

McNamara, J., and Wemple S., (1977) 'Sanctity and Power', in R. Bridenthal and C. Koony, eds, *Becoming Visible: Women in European History*, Boston, Houghton Mifflin, pp. 110–16.

Mens, A. (1958) 'Les béguines et les béghards dans le cadre de la culture médiévale', in *Moyen Age* 64, pp. 205–15.

Menzies, L. (1953), see *Texts*, above.

Mierlo, J. van, 'Béguins, Béguines, Béguinages' in *Dictionnaire de Spiritualité*, pp. 1341–52.

Moltmann-Wendel, E. (1984) 'Martha – A Forgotten Medieval Tradition', in E. Moltmann-Wendel and J. Moltmann, eds., *Humanity in God*, London, SCM.

Moore, R. I. (1975) *The Birth of Popular Heresy*. London, Edward Arnold pp. 101–11 on Lambert le Bègue.

Nelson, J. L. (1972) 'Society, Theodicy and The Origins of Heresy: Towards a Reassessment of the Medieval Evidence', Baker (1972), pp. 65–77.

Olyslager, W. A. (1983) *Het Groot Begijnhof van Leuven*. Leuven 1978; Abridged and revised English language edition, Leuven 1983.

Petroff, E. A., ed. (1986) *Medieval Women's Visionary Literature*. Oxford University Press.

Philippen, L. J. M. (1918) *De Begijnhoven, Oorsprong, Geschiedenis, Inrichtung*. Antwerp 1918.

Phillips, D. (1941) *Beguines in Medieval Strasburg: A Study of the Social Aspect of Beguine Life*. Palo Alto, Stanford University Press.

Porete, Marguerite (1981) *A Mirror for Simple Souls*. Edited, translated and adapted by Charles Crawford, Spiritual Classics Series, Dublin, Gill and Macmillan.

Power, E. E. (1922) *Medieval English Nunneries*. Cambridge University Press.

Power, E. E. (1975) *Medieval Women*. M. M. Postan, ed. Cambridge University Press.

Raitt, J., ed. (1987) *Christian Spirituality: High Middle Ages and Reformation*. London, Routledge.

Rörig, F. (1967) *The Medieval Town*. London.

Ruh, K. (1977) 'Beginenmystik: Hadewijch, Mechthild von Magdeburg, Marguerite Porete', *Zeitschrift für deutsches Altertum und deutsche Literatur* 106, pp. 265–77.

Russell, J. B. (1972) *Witchcraft in the Middle Ages*. Ithaca NY, Cornell University Press.

Schulenburg, J. T., 'Female Sanctity: Public and Private Roles, c. 500–1100', in Erler and Kowaleski (1988), pp. 102–25.

Southern, R. W. (1970) *Western Society and the Church in the Middle Ages*. Pelican History of the Church, Harmondsworth, Penguin.

Wainwright-deKadt, E. (1980) 'Courtly Literature and Mysticism: Some Aspects of their Interaction', *Acta Gemanica* 12.

Weinstein, D., and Bell, R. M. (1982) *Saints and Society: Two Worlds of Western Christendom 1000–1700*. Chicago IL, University of Chicago Press.

Wilson, I. (1988) *The Bleeding Wound*. London, Weidenfeld and Nicolson.